KIMO THEATRE

FACT & FOLKLORE

PRESENTED BY SOUTHWEST WRITERS

Jacqueline Murray Loring, Writer/Editor

© Copyright 2019 by SouthWest Writers Workshop

All rights reserved.

No part of this book may be reproduced in any form or by any electronic or mechanical means, including information storage and retrieval systems, without specific written permission from the contributors.

Rights to the individual works contained within this anthology are owned by the submitting contributors and/or their assignees. Each has permitted the use of their work in this collection.

Interior photographs contain information on persons who submitted them and locations the originals can be found.

Cover Art by Fresh Design Books. Michelle Fairbanks, Nanaimo, BC Canada https://freshdesignbooks.carbonmade.com/

Photo credit for front cover pictures
    KiMo in lights at top of cover. Circa 2017. Photo credit: Brad Stoddard.
 Photos below neon sign, left to right:
    Central Avenue. Looking east toward the Sandia Mountain. Circa 1950s. Courtesy: Albuquerque Museum and KiMo Theatre.
    KiMo Theatre. Circa 2017. Photo credit: Alexandra Dell'Amore.
    KiMo Theatre. "Thank You Albuquerque For Saving the KiMo." Circa 1970s. Courtesy: KiMo Theatre.
 Back cover. Top to bottom.
    KiMo Theatre. 1927 construction. Electricians stand on marquee. Courtesy: Albuquerque Museum and KiMo Theatre.
    Auditorium. Audience at *Pippi Longstocking*. Albuquerque Young Actors. Circa 2003. Photo credit: Rick Nickerson
    Marquee. *Steve Earl and the Dukes*. Circa 2017 Photo credit: Alexandra Dell'Amore.
    KiMo Theatre. Night performance. Circa 2017. Photo credit: Brad Stoddard.

SouthWest Writers
Carlisle Executive Offices
3200 Carlisle Blvd N.E.
Albuquerque, New Mexico 87110
www.southwestwriters.com

KiMo Theatre: Fact & Folklore
Jacqueline Murray Loring, Editor in Chief
Rose Marie Kern, Assistant Editor

ISBN-13: 978-0-9985725-2-9
Library of Congress Control Number 1-7366892161

ACCLAIM FOR THE KIMO THEATRE

"Beneath the Native American symbol for clouds, a positive sign, painted over the KiMo main stage, on a space that has been used by entertainers from Mickey Rooney to local mariachi groups to Vortex Theatre thespians performing the works of Shakespeare for middle school students, the KiMo Theatre has vibrated with the sounds and voices of a multicultural community for decades. This space has been danced on in styles from hip-hop to tap dance to Matachines. From Gilbert and Sullivan light opera to Gospel song to Buffy St. Marie's Native rock music to magic shows to Aztec dance led by PAZ (the founder and leader of Ehecatl) the magic of performing artists in the KiMo continues into the 21st century."

—*Brenda Cole, writer*

"The KiMo is uniquely New Mexico and one of the most beautiful historical theatres on Route 66. It is always a pleasure to sit in the cushy seats and look up at the great beamed ceiling and steer heads with glowing red eyes surrounding the stage."

—*Brad Stoddard, President, New Mexico Post Alliance*

"I would guess the KiMo is the crown jewel of the entire Southwestern USA when it comes to Pueblo Art Deco, which in turn means it is the pinnacle of Pueblo Deco architecture of the world!"

—*Tracy Jordan, 2017 President, Board of Directors,*
New Mexico Film Foundation

"The KiMo, the grande dame of New Mexico theatres, wears her age splendidly. I never imagined that I would stand on that graceful stage, but life has a way of handing us surprises."

—*Anne Hillerman, author*

"The KiMo Theatre is a cultural icon in our community, and throughout my time as mayor, I have made it my business to see to its improvement. This architectural treasure speaks to Albuquerque's distinct sense of place, history, and the importance we place on arts and culture in our community."

—*Richard J. Berry,*
Mayor of the City of Albuquerque 2009–2017

"The KiMo Theatre turned seventy when I was elected mayor. Little did I know that in 1953 that I would one day run the facility as Mayor! I say 1953 because I think that was around the time my best friend Mike and I ventured downtown to see *Invaders from Mars*. We were so frightened by that movie we spent most of the run time in the lobby looking at the decor. I now look back at that theatre and realize what a monumental landmark it has been for Albuquerque. Oh, that we could once again revel in the great architecture and culture that the Roaring Twenties believed was important."

—*Jim Baca, Mayor of the City of Albuquerque,*
December 1997-November 2001

"The KiMo is where I started my career. The energy of the artists who performed there somehow remains. So many performers' dreams started at the KiMo. If only the walls could talk, the stories we would hear. The KiMo will always be in my heart."

—Actor Steven Michael Quezada (*DEA Agent Steven Gomez on the Emmy Award-winning television series "Breaking Bad"*)

"Besides the beauty of the KiMo's architecture, this iconic theatre represents the City of Albuquerque's dedication to the arts and support of the community. The KiMo is as beautiful in spirit as it is in presence."

—*Dirk Norris, executive director, New Mexico Film Foundation*

"As KiMo manager, I was part of a team with local performing groups and city employees who united to work together to do shows at the KiMo Theatre to produce a living theatre. Over the years, I've had the privilege to work with many amazing artists and productions and performers and mentored young people. Theatres aren't just brick and mortar. They are alive. Part of my job as the City's community service liaison was to help make these groups and their performances successful."

—Rush Dudley,
Manager of the KiMo Theatre, 1985-2000

"Bookworks has been thrilled to partner with the KiMo over the years, especially on our Albuquerque Public Library Foundation series, *A Word with Writers*, which opened to a sold-out crowd with George RR Martin and Diana Gabaldon in May 2014. We've also hosted many other best-selling and award-winning authors at the KiMo, too much success, including Alexander McCall Smith, Anne Hillerman, Jacqueline Woodson, and Brian Cranston. The Brian Cranston event was a night none of us will probably ever forget, replete with red carpet and the stars of *Breaking Bad* taking the stage after his talk with Bob Odenkirk. Larry Parker is an absolute gem to the city; he always pulls together an amazing crew and works our events with a smile."

—Amanda Sutton,
Events and Marketing Director, Bookworks

"We've had the pleasure of being hosted at the KiMo for our annual *Movies & Meaning Festival* for three years now (2015-2018). We've screened beautiful films in the elegant surroundings, had conversations with folk like Alice Walker, Malidoma Somé, Mona Haydar, Godfrey Reggio, and Rodrigo Garcia, and nurtured a community dedicated to making a better world through telling better stories.

There are venues that offer good technical equipment and a decent place to work, but the KiMo is special. Not only is it a magnificent space that gets better with age, but the folk who work there make it feel like a home away from home. Here's to the next 90 years."

—Gareth Higgins,
Movies & Meaning Festival

"I loved the KiMo Theatre from the moment I stepped into it as an audience member. That was a full ten years before AirDance New Mexico's first aerial art performance."

—Debra Landau,
Artistic Director, AirDance New Mexico

Dancing, theatre, music, poetry, that's the KiMo today."

—Rudy J. Miera, author of
"The Fall and Rise of Champagne Sanchez"

Missing Information
About the History of the KiMo Theatre

As you read this book or tour the KiMo Theatre, look closely at the photographs or posters. If you recognize a person in a photo, can date an event, or know the photographer, please take a moment to give that information to a KiMo staff. Your information will add to the KiMo history.

Mr. and Mrs. Bachechi. Circa 1927. Courtesy: KiMo Theatre.
Photo credit: JMLoring

This book is dedicated to

Oreste Bachechi and his wife, Maria Franceschi Bachechi for their dream in the 1920s of a picture palace in Downtown Albuquerque and their vision and tenacity to build the KiMo Theatre.

The Bachechi children and their children's children's children for keeping that dream alive.

And

The citizens of the City of Albuquerque, who from 1977 to May 2019 have invested in and participated in the KiMo's history, preservation, renovation, performances, and events and who continue to envision an even more wondrous, inclusive, flamboyant, drama-filled future for the KiMo Theatre.

KIMO THEATRE: FACT & FOLKLORE
TABLE OF CONTENTS

Page

15 Introduction by Jacqueline Murray Loring (JMLoring)
16 Book Layout Guide
20 Important Personages Referred to in the Writing of this Book

Section One

The History of the KiMo Theatre from 1927-2017

25 Naming the KiMo   JMLoring
  • Comments about Pablo Abeita   Verna Williamson-Teller
29 The City of Albuquerque and the KiMo Theatre   Rush Dudley
33 A Grand Beginning   Brenda Cole
  • More on the Theatre's Name
  • Mrs. Bachechi and the KiMo
38 The Bachechi Family & the KiMo Theatre   JMLoring
  • Finding Adelina Timofeyew
  • The Pole Sitter
51 The KiMo Theatre, 1920s and Silent Film   Brenda Cole
59 Competition for the KiMo   JMLoring
  • Growth and Change in Albuquerque
65 KiMo Theatre's Jug Band Alley   Barbara Piper
67 Restoration and Renovation after 1977   Rush Dudley
71 The KiMo and Me: Protecting the KiMo Theatre   David Rusk
81 The Grand Reopening 1928   Rudy J. Miera
  • *Nuevo Mexico, Si!*
  • KiMo Folklore
  • La Compania de Teatro de Alburquerque
  • Kalpulli Ehecatl Aztec Dancers
  • The Night of the Re-opening
93 The KiMo in the New Millennium 2000-2017   JMLoring

Section Two

The Personal Impact of the Theatre

103	Memories of Rick Rhodes & Margo Radaelli	Dianne R. Layden
107	A Paranormal Place	JMLoring
109	Bobby: The Spirit of the KiMo	Connie Spiegel
113	New Mexico Young Actors-Nickerson	Rick Nickerson
117	New Mexico Young Actors-Bower	Paul Bower
123	Growing Up at the KiMo	David Zamora
124	The Ballet Repertory Theater Preamble	JMLoring
125	Ballet Repertory Theater	Katherine Giese
131	Managing the KiMo	Rush Dudley
134	A Celebration of Unity 1992	JMLoring
147	An Albuquerque Poet Remembers	Don McIver
150	Twilight in the KiMo Theatre	Pamela Yenser
153	The Grande Dame	Anne Hillerman
155	The Alvarado Follies	Mary E. Dorsey
157	Opera Southwest	Tony Zancanella
161	Books, Film and Fame	JMLoring
163	The Duke City Shootout	Anthony DellaFlora
175	Planning the 90th Anniversary	JMLoring

Section Three
The Tour of the KiMo Theatre

187	The Grand Exterior	JMLoring
191	Construction Influences	JMLoring
193	Redeeming Swastikas	Sam Moorman
197	Native American Influences	Kathy Wagoner
201	Starting Your Walking Tour	JMLoring

- The Neon Sign
- The Ticket Office Lobby
- Sally Rand
- Glass Cases & Memorabilia Posters of Silent Films
- Gordon Church
- Mary McKinney, Popcorn, & WWII
- Theatre Lobby
- Crossover Aisle Drawings
- Painters and Exhibits
- The Wurlitzer Pipe Organ
- Albuquerque Museum Displays the KiMo Organ & Ticket Box
- The Proscenium Arch
- Theater Fire Curtain
- Continuing Renovations
- Projection Booth, Projector and Projectionist
- The New Silver Screen

237	Theatre Seats 1971	Laura Sundt Pierce
240	Accommodating the Opera	Sally Opel & Stewart Dawson
247	AirDance Stage Modification	Debra Landau
251	Stairway, Handrail, Balcony, Mezzanine	JMLoring
257	City of Albuquerque Saves the KiMo Theatre	
259	Carl Von Hassler's Murals	JMLoring
261	The Missing Paintings	Jeff Benham
265	First Run Movie Posters-Mezzanine	JM Loring
273	The End of the Tour	

275   Acknowledgements

280   Author Biography – Jacqueline Murray Loring

283   Index

In addition to sections being written by various individuals, the book also contains commentaries by Rochelle Bussey, Mathew Carter, Dana Feldman, Sharon Higgins, Fran Krukar, Ann Lerner, Larry Parker, Steven Michael Quezada, Brad Stoddard, Mapitzmitl Xiukwetzpaltzin (PAZ).

Introduction

By Jacqueline Murray Loring

When I was asked in 2017 by the board of SouthWest Writers to head the project to write a book celebrating the 90th anniversary of the KiMo Theatre, I was a newcomer to Albuquerque and to the KiMo Theatre. I had attended several films shown at the theatre sponsored by the 48 Hour Film Project, Indie Q, and the Albuquerque Film and Music Experience.

I'd heard the theatre, located at 423 Central Avenue, Route 66, mentioned in conversations with screenwriters about the *Duke City Shootout*. I knew nothing about its origin, history, national fame, or the historical and sentimental value it holds for the community of Albuquerque. The KiMo Theatre is more than a building that showed first-run silent films back in the Roaring Twenties, more than an auditorium that can be rented by an individual or organization, and more than a space to hold a high school graduation.

For ninety years, hundreds of thousands of adults and children have packed the KiMo theatre to watch ballet, drama, spoken-word, and to listen to poetry readings. Performers have acted, sung, danced, and spellbound audiences with magic. Local filmmakers flock there to watch their indie films come alive on the new silver screen. The KiMo continues to host movie premieres and vintage film festivals.

Book Layout Guide
Section 1 - The History of the KiMo Theatre from 1927 to 2018

This section contains a broad spectrum of Facts, Fiction, and Folklore about the Theatre including newly-told stories, articles, memoirs, insights, opinions, never-before-heard remembrances, and researched facts about the KiMo Theatre as a performing arts theatre and a movie palace. This collection was written by people who, over the years, have developed and nurtured a loving, respectful relationship with the theatre.

Past employees, elected officials, performers, and audience members share remembrances of the Bachechi family, the theatre's construction in 1927, the 1977 vote by Albuquerque citizens to buy and preserve the building, the theatre's closings for renovations, its murals, art, and (and disputed) paranormal activity.

Here you will find passed-down family folklore and anecdotes that reflect the rich, flamboyant, and diverse cultural life inside the theatre, and the impact the KiMo has had on the lives of the people who have supported it for ninety years. These personal insights are a lens which reveals the broader and deeper story of the theatre.

Included is an account written by an Isleta Tribal elder about the relationship between Oreste Bachechi and Pablo Abeita, and a tale told by a man who first danced with his father on stage at the KiMo as a child. An author writes about her first visit and how she was charmed and intrigued by the KiMo Theatre's ambiance. Teachers write about the impact of attending performances with students and parents. An article about a KiMo staff member whose work at the KiMo touched members of the Albuquerque community is an example of how life at the KiMo is not insular. One essay is the personal, tragic, but hilarious story that demonstrates occasional confusion when the name KiMo is spoken but not written.

Memories included in *KiMo Theatre: Fact & Folklore* have passed from one generation to a younger generation to today's theatre-goers. Some early and present-day tales may be true, but others may only be true in the storyteller's story. Some facts are still being researched.

Many of the photographs in this book have been preserved by museums, universities, the City of Albuquerque, and the KiMo Theatre itself. Their use was donated to SouthWest Writers for publication in this book.

Section 2
Memories: The Personal Impact of the Theatre

The comprehensive history of the KiMo Theatre must include stories about the iconic building, the people who worked there, and the audiences who were enriched by attending events. But there is more to the KiMo story. There are stories to be told of the impact the theatre has had for ninety years on members of the Albuquerque community. Included in this book is an article by writer and SouthWest Writers member Dianne R. Layden. Layden's memory of Margot Radaelli and Rick Rhodes and Rick's impact on his friends and community tells the story of the KiMo through the broadest lens.

Section 3
Official History and Tour Guide

Here you will find the official history of the museum along with a guided tour anyone reading the book can take. The KiMo Theatre is a historic landmark available for guided and self-guided tours. Through storytelling, this book provides the reader with a ninety-year history of the theatre and acts as an insider's handbook to guide you along your tour of the building itself.

Our Wish for the Reader

It is the hope of SouthWest Writers and the people who worked on this project and are listed in the acknowledgments section, that this book will capture your imagination, provide insight into years long past, inform, educate, and provide a fun path for exploration. KiMo Theatre buffs will find it a treasure trove of new and clarified information and a valuable resource to further explore the history of the theatre. At the end of the book internet links are provided to readers who wish to continue to research historical facts, photographs, or people.

Please know that the opinions and memories expressed in this book by performers, audience members, officials, KiMo employees, community members, and interested bystanders are theirs and do not necessarily reflect those of SouthWest Writers, or this editor/writer. All the narratives have been included with great delight as written by their authors. The writer and editors of this book have noted some important differences when they occur in the text as [Editor's note]. Occasionally, words with more than one spelling or interpretation are identified for the reader including the original spelling of

Alburquerque vs. the present-day spelling of Albuquerque, Pass Time Theatre vs. Pastime Theatre, Maria Bachechi vs. Mary Bachechi. There is a detailed description of the difference between and significance of the words Tiva or Teva.

The KiMo Theatre is more than a concrete building, more than a performing arts center, and more than a meeting place for friends. The KiMo Theatre is a symbol of the endurance of a dream. It is a living, breathing, growing part of Albuquerque, fully the sum of its historical, cultural, spiritual, artistic, and community parts.

—Jacqueline Murray Loring, April 2018

NOTE: All sections of the book not directly attributed to a different author were researched and written by Jacqueline Murray Loring (JMLoring)

KiMo Theatre

Important Personages Referred to in the Writing of this Book

Jim Baca, Mayor of the City of Albuquerque, 1997 - 2001

Richard J. Berry, Mayor of the City of Albuquerque, 2009 - 2017

Paul Bower, Current Director, New Mexico Young Actors

Alan Clarke, Appointed KiMo manager by the City of 1977

Rush Dudley, Manager of KiMo Theatre, 1985-2000

Katherine Giese, Current Director, Ballet Repertory Theatre

Rudy J. Miera, Author and Historian

Rick Nickerson, Founder of New Mexico Young Actors

Larry Parker, Manager of KiMo Theatre from 2008 to present

Barbara Piper, Member of the Watermelon Mountain Jug Band

David Rusk, Mayor of Albuquerque 1977-1981

Brad Stoddard, President of Post-Alliance, Film organization

Verna Williamson-Teller, Governor of the Isleta Pueblo from 1987 to 1990

KiMo Theatre. Circa 2017.
Photo credit: Alexandra Dell'Amore

Native Languages

Among the nineteen New Mexico pueblos many languages are spoken:
Tiwa is spoken by the members of the Pueblos of Isleta, Picuris, Sandia, and Taos. Tewa is spoken by the people of the Santa Clara, Nambé, Pojoaque, Tesuque, San Ildefonso, and Ohkay Owingeh (San Juan) Pueblos.

The Keresan (Kewa) language is spoken by the Acoma, Cochiti, Laguna, San Felipe, Santa Ana, Santa Domingo, and Zia Pueblos.

Towa is spoken by members of the Jemez Pueblo.

The Zuni Pueblo people speak the Zuni language.

SECTION I

THE HISTORY OF THE KIMO THEATRE FROM 1927 TO 2018.

KiMo (pronounced kee-mo)

Tiwa Pueblo Language

"Mountain Lion"

Naming the KiMo Theatre

By Jacqueline Murray Loring

After ninety years, the KiMo has generated thousands of remembrances and some legends. Many New Mexico theatre history buffs and Albuquerque residents can recite by heart the facts surrounding the naming of the KiMo. A contest, they will tell you. Won by the Isleta Pueblo governor. But king vs. lion vs. mountain?

The grand opening of the KiMo Theatre was on September 19, 1927. A contest had been held by Mr. Oreste Bachechi, the Theatre's builder, to name the new theatre and was won by Isleta Pueblo Governor Pablo Abeita. He combined two words in the Tiwa language meaning 'mountain lion.' The opening night performance was a complete sellout. The audience was captivated by Native Americans from several pueblos who performed their dances, accompanied by singers and drumming. A copy of the original program is on file at the University of New Mexico's main library, and photos of the event are available at the KiMo, the University of New Mexico Library, and the Albuquerque Museum.

Larry Parker has been the manager of the KiMo Theatre for over ten years. He is respected as the official historian of the theatre. "By default," he will tell you. "Only because I've been here the longest." Parker was asked for his understanding of the history behind how the KiMo Theatre was named, the importance of the spelling KiMo, and whether the parts of the words meant king of the mountain. If "Ki" meant King and if "Mo" was meant to stand for mountain lion.

Parker said, "I don't know the truth of why the word KiMo is spelled the way it is. The story I was told when I got this job years ago was that when the Bachechi's ran the contest in 1927, Pablo Abeita, who was then the governor of the Isleta Pueblo, submitted the name KiMo to Oreste. And, I assume all these years later that the name was spelled that way when it was submitted. The interesting parts of the stories I hear about the naming is that the urban myths that have filtered down over ninety years say that the name is a combination of "king of its kind or mountain lion. I gave a tour of the KiMo a few years back to the great-granddaughter of Governor Abeita. She said she was kind of confused too. Because as far as she could recall, there is no word for king in the Tiwa dialect. A lot of KiMo information, stories, and folklore have filtered down, filtered through after ninety years. Where the truth is …?"

Comments by Verna Williamson-Teller about Pablo Abeita

Verna Williamson-Teller was governor of the Isleta Pueblo from 1987 to 1990. She recalls as a child hearing stories about the friendship between Pablo Abeita and his wife and Oreste and Maria Bachechi.

Pablo Abeita (1871–1940) graduated from St. Michael's College in Santa Fe and spoke both Tiwa and English. Besides serving as Governor of the Isleta Pueblo, he was a business man, an interrupter, and diplomat. Mrs. Williamson-Teller said, "Pablo Abeita was friends with Teddy Roosevelt, who visited him at the Isleta Pueblo with Mr. Bachechi. There was a strong connection among Pueblo peoples with the people of the Gutierrez-Hubbell family, the Atrisco Land Grant people, and the Bachechis. I remember people talking about the event when I was a child, all those years later. When the KiMo theatre was built, it was built with a lot of Pueblo influences. It appeared that Mr. Abeita had alot to do with the design and the décor. I wouldn't doubt that Pueblo handiwork is in there. Mr. Abeita and his wife were invited to the KiMo when they were opening it up. He named it."

Williamson-Teller clarifies the spelling and pronunciation of the word KiMo this way. "The Isleta language is a spoken language, not a written one. When Pablo Abeita named the theatre the word he used was a Tiwa word and it was adapted to the English form. The sound of the Isleta word is more closely pronounced "khim oo, a softer "k" sound than the way it is pronounced by non-Native people. The word was anglicized to KiMo. When spelled out and pronounced phonetically, it has the hard sound of the letter "K". It is one word to mean mountain lion, not two words broken into khim, meaning mountain and oo meaning lion.

The Isleta word (KiMo) means mountain lion. We have people here in New Mexico whose name is Kimo and there's a Kimo Construction company, spelled with a lower case "M" and pronounced the Tiwa way. We don't have lions here in New Mexico. We do have cougars. Sometimes they would be referred to as mountain lions. Some non-Indians refer to the lion as king. We don't have kings, we are not a monarchy so that term doesn't come from the Pueblos. If we used the word king, we would use the Spanish word "rey". Pablo Abeita, having been educated in the east, may have used the term "King" to describe the mountain lion, something that his non-Indian friends could relate to. That might be where the confusion came in.

The City of Albuquerque and the KiMo Theatre

by Rush Dudley

Rush Dudley was the Manager of the KiMo Theatre from 1985 to 2000

In the early days of the 1920s, 1930s, 1940s, Downtown Albuquerque was thriving. The KiMo Theatre was part of its rich social life. People got dressed up to go to movies or stage shows. They went to dinner, strolled down the main streets, met their neighbors, and stopped to have conversations. In the late 1920s and 1930s, there was a trolley system between Albuquerque Old Town and New Town (Downtown) and a lot of building going up to service the railroad. And the new people! Big-time building; the KiMo, First National Bank, and the Sunshine Theatre. Albuquerque's Old Town Plaza was the agricultural center settled by the families that came up through the Valley and New Town was the railroad industrial center.

The original State Fair (Territorial Fair 1890) was held west of Albuquerque (Old Town), toward the river. The Pueblos would participate with dances. The first fairs had a large Native American participation. There were dances and a big parade. The Native Americans would bring in horses and ride in the parade from Albuquerque to Old Town to New Town on Central Avenue in full Native regalia. Cowboys would dress up, ride, and rodeo. The fair presented goods and products of the three New Mexico cultures. The parade developed into the All-American Parade, and the KiMo Theatre would do up a float.

In the 1920s and 1930s, Albuquerque presented beauty contests. The beauty pageant was held to choose a queen. They'd hold it on the KiMo's stage and do photographs at Tingley Beach.

For the KiMo's 70th (1996-1997) anniversary celebration, two of the Bachechi sons came to the KiMo and I talked to them. One told me the story about their father, Oreste.

Oreste Bachechi was fourteen years old when he got on a ship in Italy with his three brothers to immigrate to America. The way you did it in those days was to go through Mexico. At the dock in Mexico, he got separated from his brothers. The sons had no information about Oreste's brothers except that he never saw them again.

One way to make money in those days was to set up a tent and sell goods and probably beer to the railroad workers. That's how he got his start, with a tent. Over the years, he prospered. The Italian community grew too.

Oreste Bachechi initiated the process by which large numbers of Italians came to Albuquerque after hearing about the city. There are lots of Italian names in Albuquerque. You can just look at the names on the buildings around town: grocery stores, supply houses, apartments.

You can see the remnants downtown. The Bachechis had a dry goods store. They owned several houses. They bought a house on Nob Hill. Made a compound. After Mr. Bachechi died, Mrs. (Maria) Bachechi remained active and powerful her whole life. She ran the businesses and was a major contributor to the Albuquerque community."

KiMo Theatre. 1927 construction.
Courtesy: Albuquerque Museum and KiMo Theatre.

KiMo Theatre. 1927 construction. Electricians stand on marquee.
Courtesy: Albuquerque Museum and KiMo Theatre

KiMo Theatre. 1927 construction.
Courtesy: Albuquerque Museum and KiMo Theatre

A Grand Beginning

by Brenda Cole

Brenda Cole is an author, editor, and SouthWest Writers member

It was the 1920s and America was hoppin'.

The War to end all Wars was over, hemlines had risen and the time was ripe for a new venue for entertainment. An immigrant couple from Italy was finally ready to bring a new light to Albuquerque, New Mexico.

Oreste Bachechi and Maria (Mary) Franceschi Bachechi arrived in Albuquerque in 1884. They were quite the industrious pair and by the 1920s they had prospered; seven kids and the Bachechi Dry Goods store run by Maria and Mrs. Armida Napoleone over on North First Street.

Oreste and two of his sons, (Arthur and Lawrence), owned and managed the Anchor Milling and Grocery Company on New York Street by the railroad tracks. However, Oreste's real love was the theatre. He and Maria set up the Bachechi Amusement Company and by 1919 they were the proprietors of the *Past Time Theatre* and the *New Indian Theatre* along with their partner, Joe Barnett. Their son, Victor, was the manager.

Things went well for the next six years, but Oreste wasn't satisfied. He wanted his own theatre, a movie "palace" made to his specifications. He wanted something grand, different and one that would stand out among all the other theatres of the time.

In 1925, Oreste began the formation of his dream. He contracted with Carl Boller to design and build his vision of a theatre for Albuquerque. Boller was with Boller Brothers Architectural Company out of Los Angeles, California. The Bachechi's had chosen wisely. They envisioned a grand palace done in a Southwestern motif which would showcase the artistic styles native to New Mexico. The Boller firm had designed several theatres across the country. After an extended research period and a trip through New Mexico's pueblos, Boller drafted a unique design combining elements of Art Deco and Pueblo styles.

Funding for the venture was a bit tricky. Local bankers were reluctant to extend funds, so the loan was finally obtained from investors in Chicago. $150,000 was spent building the theatre, with construction being completed in less than one year.

One of the larger expenses was for the enormous Wurlitzer pipe organ that was installed. Silent movies would have an organist or orchestra play along with the film for atmosphere. The organ alone would cost $18,000.

More on The Theatre's Name

The Grand Opening of the KiMo Theatre was on September 19, 1927. Mr. Bachechi held a contest to name the new theatre. It was won by Isleta Pueblo Governor, Pablo Abieta.

The opening night performance was a complete sellout. The audience was captivated by tribal members of several local pueblos performing their dances accompanied by singers and drumming.

A copy of the original program is on file at the University of New Mexico's main library, and photos of the event are available at the KiMo, the University of New Mexico Library, and the Albuquerque Museum." [More about the naming of the KiMo Theatre in Section II-The Tour.]

Mayor Clyde Tingley congratulates Bachechi Amusement Company. Circa 1927. Courtesy: KiMo Theatre.

Mrs. Bachechi and the KiMo

September 19, 1927 was the beginning of an important era for Albuquerque. Oreste Bachechi had triumphed. The KiMo Theatre, his grand dream, was built as he envisioned. It was a roaring success.

But Bachechi did not live long enough to enjoy his accomplishment. Sadly, just after the KiMo opened, Mr. Bachechi became ill and died in early 1928. His death came as a shock to his friends in the city. With his passing, the family shifted to cover the loss of their patriarch.

The 1928 Albuquerque City Directory lists three people as proprietors of the KiMo and Pastime theatres: "Mary Bachechi and her sons Arthur and Victor. Two of her other sons also worked in the family business. Lawrence was listed as a machine operator for the Pastime and Mario as the assistant manager there. Bachechi's wife and sons carried on his movie palace dream, which in the 1920s and 1930s included a schedule of silent movies, vaudeville, burlesque and traveling road shows."

The Pastime Theatre

The text with a photograph of the Pastime Theatre archived at the University of New Mexico states:

Title: Pastime Theatre, ca. 1924
Creator: Ciotola, Nicholas P.; Timofeyew, Adelina
Subject: Italian Americans; Albuquerque (N.M.) -- History; Business enterprises -- New Mexico -- Albuquerque; Albuquerque (N.M.) -- Theatres

Description: Oreste Bachechi, an Italian immigrant who had built his fortune in liquor distribution, became the proprietor of the Pastime Theatre at 213 West Central Avenue with the onset of prohibition in 1919.

(Photo courtesy of Adelina Timofeyew.)
Collection: Nicholas P. Ciotola Italians in Albuquerque Pictorial Collection.

http://econtent.unm.edu/cdm/search/collection/Ciotola/searchterm/Pastime%20Theatre/order/title

Bachechi Family and the KiMo Theatre

by Jacqueline Murray Loring

The Center for Southwest Research, University Libraries, at the University of New Mexico is a godsend to researchers looking to educate themselves photographically with the history of Albuquerque, Albuquerque's Italian heritage, and the history of the KiMo Theatre. The research for this book began with a caption and the related photograph found it that collection.

Another Center for Southwest Research photograph stated "Oreste Bachech owned the Pastime Theatre before he built the KiMo." Another said Mr. (Luigi) Puccini also owned that theatre [Pastime] at a later time. Many of the photos in the collection contained the attribution "Photo courtesy of Adelina Timofeyew".

Even with these pieces of information as starting points, the KiMo Theatre's path from 1929 to 2017 was filled with false trails. At this early discovery point, the significance of the name "Adelina Timofeyew," was unknown to this writer but clearly her donation of New Mexico photographs with text were essential to researching Albuquerque's history and to the story of the KiMo Theatre. This series of photographs and hundreds of others are available to researchers on-line and at the library.

Finding Adelina Timofeyew

While searching for information about the public and KiMo Theatre-centered lives of Oreste and Maria Bachechi, I discovered discrepancies among published sources. Simple facts like the number of living children Mr. and Mrs. Bachechi parented differed. According to their great-granddaughter, Ekaterina Puccini Timofeyew, there were six children. Many news articles report the names of their sons and their accomplishments, especially as they worked to keep the KiMo Theatre vital. Nowhere in my early research did I discover that the Bachechis had a daughter. It was months later when I found an obituary of Virginia Doyle by *Albuquerque Journal* staff writer Lloyd Jojola in which he interviewed Doyle's niece, Ekaterina Puccini Timofeyew. She said she was the great-granddaughter of Maria Bachechi. The Bachechis daughter, Iole, was the oldest Bachechi child. The dominos began to fall into place.

Iole Bachechi (1892-1973) married Luigi Puccini (1888-1972) in 1914. Theirs is a truly charming story of love and vision. See the link to their story at the end of this section.

A quick look at Mr. Puccini's business history shows that in the 1920s, he bought the Pastime Theatre in Albuquerque. Later, he owned the Gem Theatre in Durango, Colorado and the Rex Theatre in Gallup, New Mexico. In 1929, Mr. Puccini built a grocery store that became Puccini's Golden West Saloon, located at 620 Central Avenue.

In the 1940s, he built the El Rey Theatre at 622 Central Avenue as a movie theatre. The KiMo is located at 423 Central Avenue, across the street and a block from these establishments. Iole and Luigi had three children: a son, Oreste Puccini, Jr., and two daughters, Virginia Puccini Doyle and Adelina Puccini Timofeyew. Ekaterina Puccini Timofeyew is Adelina's daughter. Adelina is a composer, singer, and musician. According to Ekaterina Puccini Timofeyew, among her early accomplishments, Virginia was a dancer and trapeze artist who appeared with the Ringling Brothers and Barnum & Bailey Circus.

In the 1980s, Iole Bachechi Puccini's daughters, Adelina and Virginia, took over the running of the El Rey Theatre and what became known as Puccini's Golden West. In February 2008, Puccini's was consumed by fire, but the El Rey was spared. Ekaterina Puccini Timofeyew, daughter of Adelina, granddaughter of Iole, and the great-granddaughter of Maria Bachechi, is the owner of the El Rey building. A concert by world-renowned cellist Matt Haimovitz was scheduled for the El Rey the day after the fire but was relocated to the KiMo Theatre.

I mention these Puccini facts in a book about the KiMo Theatre because in the general history of Albuquerque, the history of entertainment in Albuquerque, and the specific history of the KiMo Theatre, this extended family matters.

For more in-depth information about the El Rey Theatre or Puccini's Golden West Saloon fire in Ekaterina Puccini Timofeyew's own words, see:
- https://www.bizjournals.com/albuquerque/stories/2007/11/05/story11.html
- https://www.abqjournal.com/obits/profiles/20225636profiles02-20-10.htm
- https://www.abqjournal.com/news/metro/291702metro03-07-08.htm
- https://www.abqjournal.com/news/metro/289412metro02-29-08.htm

Mr. Bachechi and the Pole Sitter

As an Albuquerque newcomer writing a book about the KiMo Theatre, it was essential to verify facts with a wide variety of local experts. Glenn Fye is the photo archivist at the Albuquerque Museum. During hours of viewing and researching the history behind some of the museum's photography collection with him, one photograph was especially intriguing.

It is a wide-angle view of the KiMo Theatre and Central Avenue at the intersection with Fifth Street taken between 1927 and 1928. When enlarged, this photo clearly shows the front and the roof of the KiMo building. A group of well-dressed folks stand in the street. An enthusiastic young man appears to stand on a brand-new car.

I titled this photo, "Man Standing on Car".

KiMo Theatre. Man standing on car. Cropped photograph.
Circa 1927. Courtesy: Albuquerque Museum and KiMo Theatre.

KiMo Theatre. Man standing on car. Wide shot.
Circa 1927. Courtesy: Albuquerque Museum and KiMo Theatre.

A second Albuquerque Museum picture of the same event appears to have been taken moments before or after the first. The photographs are similar but different including the people photographed. In the second photograph, a close-up, the jovial man is not standing but sits casually on top of the car, his crossed legs dangling down over the driver's window. This photo I titled, "Man Sitting on Car".

KiMo Theatre. Man sitting on car. Circa 1927.
Courtesy: Albuquerque Museum and KiMo Theatre.

Unfortunately, these two photographs do not reveal the names of the people in the picture, the date the pictures were taken, or the reason the people posed for the photograph. The quest to find the historically correct answers to these questions, especially the identity of the man standing on the car, became a separate project while the rest of this book worked toward completion. The photographs are included in this book courtesy of the Museum.

Research for the facts behind the photos "man standing on car" "man sitting on car" led me to Mrs. Adelina Timofeyew, Ekaterina Puccini Timofeyew, and Rush Dudley.

Benny Fox and the Chandler Six

When asked, Rush Dudley, the KiMo Theatre manager from 1985 to 2000, thought the guy standing on the car was a famous pole sitter. No one else had mentioned that odd fact. With photograph in hand, backtracking through other sources about the possibility of an event at the KiMo that featured a pole sitter, no one mentioned that in the first picture you can clearly see a pole on the roof of the KiMo.

Though initially no one but Dudley knew about a pole sitter, I was repeatedly reassured that the picture was a Bachechi family portrait. Mr. Oreste Bachechi posing with his KiMo employees. Some theorized that the clown on the car was some crazy employee or maybe even a Bachechi son. But others said the group of people on the right of the picture were Mr. Bachechi's wife and his family.

Mrs. Adelina Timofeyew said that the woman in the hat and scarf might be her grandmother and the men might be Bachechi sons. The man was not her great-grandfather, Oreste Bachechi.

The September 10, 1928 *Albuquerque Journal* front-page solved the pole sitter mystery. The Journal's headline reads: "Benny Fox Ascends Pole". "To Sit on Pole for 100 Hours Atop the KiMo". In part the article says "fresh prepared food" in consultation with a local doctor would be sent up to Benny by rope, and "New Mexico's leading newspaper is only satisfied when it can secure the best. In Benny Fox, ninety-eight-pound wonder, international performer, the unchallenged champion is here."

And, "Upon his arrival here, Mr. Fox was met by some of the Duke City's most prominent business men. Roy Burns, Chandler distributor, and T. H. Morgan, Chandler sales manager here, presented Benny with a new Chandler Six for his exclusive (driving) use during his stay in Albuquerque. Mr. Fox is the owner and great lover of the Chandler Six and declares it is the 'real car for safety and comfort.'"

Benny Fox ascends pole.
Front page. *Albuquerque Journal*. Circa 1927.
Courtesy: *Albuquerque Journal*.

TO SIT ON POLE ATOP KIMO FOR 100 HOURS

Continued from Page one

leading restaurants. They selected the Court Cafe.

The Court Cafe has appointed a special waitress to carry fresh, Court Cafe prepared food, to Benny. It will be sent up by rope to him. The menu is prepared in consultation with Dr. J. W. Hilton, Nano Fox and Robert Katsavis, owner and manager of the Court Cafe.

Benny Fox has started his training. He feels confident he will be in perfect condition on Wednesday afternoon, September 17, when his long grind is to start. His training includes three hours of road work each day, four hours of special exercise, one hour of swimming, special massages and plenty of sleep.

Benny has been a performer and stunt artist for seventeen years and made his first parachute jump when he was ten years old.

His father and even his grandfather were stunt performers. His sister was an acrobat with Ringling Brothers for many years.

Benny Fox is known throughout the United States and Europe. Many of his feats have been the most daring and death-defying ever accomplished.

His Great Feat

One of his greatest stunts, through which he is remembered by many, was his "cable walk" across the Milwaukee river. Twenty-eight hundred feet of steel cable was drawn across the river, four hundred feet above the surface. Benny made it, as he has always made it.

Last week Benny was in El Paso. Twenty-five thousand people, approximately, witnessed his descent from the flagpole atop the Hussman hotel there.

New Mexico's leading newspaper is only satisfied when it can secure the best. In Benny Fox, ninety-eight pound wonder international performer, the unchallenged champion is here.

From Albuquerque, Benny goes to Phoenix and then to Hollywood, where he has a contract that starts with one of the leading motion picture producers.

Upon his arrival here, Mr. Fox was met by some of the Duke City's most prominent business men. Roy Burns, Chandler distributer and T. H. Morgan, Chandler sales manager here, presented Benny with a new Chandler Six for his exclusive use during his stay in Albuquerque.

A Chandler Car

Mr. Fox is an owner and great lover of the Chandler Six and declares it is "the real car for safety and comfort." During leisure hours between training schedules he will motor over Albuquerque and the surrounding country in his Chandler.

From the "doubters" will be removed their doubt and from the skeptical their skepticism, for Benny will sit his perch atop the steel pole with many spotlights playing upon him through the nights. He offers $100 to anyone who catches him off his perch during the feat. He is one of the country's highest paid performers.

Sunday Mr. and Mrs. Fox motored over the city, accompanied by Chandler officials.

Benny Fox ascends pole.

Inside page. *Albuquerque Journal*. Circa 1927. Courtesy: *Albuquerque Journal*.

Benny offered $500 to anyone who caught him off his perch during the 100 hours.

No one did.

And, "Upon his arrival here, Mr. Fox was met by some of the Duke City's most prominent business men. Roy Burns, Chandler distributor, and T. H. Morgan, Chandler sales manager here, presented Benny with a new Chandler Six for his exclusive (driving) use during his stay in Albuquerque. Mr. Fox is the owner and great lover of the Chandler Six and declares it is the 'real car for safety and comfort.'"

Benny Fox ascends pole.
Front page. *Albuquerque Journal*. Circa 1927.
Courtesy: *Albuquerque Journal*.

TO SIT ON POLE ATOP KIMO FOR 100 HOURS

Continued from Page One

leading restaurants. They selected the Court Cafe.

The Court Cafe has appointed a special waitress to carry fresh, Court Cafe prepared food, to Benny. It will be sent up by rope to him. The menu is prepared in consultation with Dr. J. W. Hilton, Nano Fox and Robert Katsavis, owner and manager of the Court Cafe.

Benny Fox has started his training. He feels confident he will be in perfect condition on Wednesday afternoon, September 17, when his long grind is to start. His training includes three hours of road work each day, four hours of special exercise, one hour of swimming, special massages and plenty of sleep.

Benny has been a performer and stunt artist for seventeen years and made his first parachute jump when he was ten years old.

His father and even his grandfather were stunt performers. His sister was an acrobat with Ringling Brothers for many years.

Benny Fox is known throughout the United States and Europe. Many of his feats have been the most daring and death-defying ever accomplished.

His Great Feat

One of his greatest stunts, through which he is remembered by many, was his "cable walk" across the Milwaukee river. Twenty-eight hundred feet of steel cable was drawn across the river, four hundred feet above the surface. Benny made it, as he has always made it.

Last week Benny was in El Paso. Twenty-five thousand people, approximately, witnessed his descent from the flagpole atop the Huseman hotel there.

New Mexico's leading newspaper is only satisfied when it can secure the best. In Benny Fox, ninety-eight pound wonder international performer, the unchallenged champion is here.

From Albuquerque, Benny goes to Phoenix and then to Hollywood, where he has a contract that starts with one of the leading motion picture producers.

Upon his arrival here, Mr. Fox was met by some of the Duke City's most prominent business men. Roy Burns, Chandler distributer and T. H. Morgan, Chandler sales manager here, presented Benny with a new Chandler Six for his exclusive use during his stay in Albuquerque.

A Chandler Car

Mr. Fox is an owner and great lover of the Chandler Six and declares it is "The real car for safety and comfort." During leisure hours between training schedules he will motor over Albuquerque and the surrounding country in his Chandler.

From the "doubters" will be removed their doubt and from the skeptical their skepticism, for Benny will sit his perch atop the steel pole with many spotlights playing upon him through the nights. He offers $100 to anyone who catches him off his perch during the feat. He is one of the country's highest paid performers.

Sunday Mr. and Mrs. Fox motored over the city, accompanied by Chandler officials.

Benny Fox ascends pole.

Inside page. *Albuquerque Journal*. Circa 1927. Courtesy: *Albuquerque Journal*.

Benny offered $500 to anyone who caught him off his perch during the 100 hours.

No one did.

Verifying Dates

Verifying the people, places and the date of the photographs of the man standing or sitting on the car came down to "fact vs. the yet unprovable." In the Albuquerque Museum photographs, the movie announced on the marquee is *Hot Heels*. The date of this movie's premiere was May 13, 1928. The *Albuquerque Journal* article was published on September 10, 1928. Information about the pole sitter found in an archived edition of the *Journal* states the newspaper sponsored the pole sitter's time on the roof of the KiMo building. The *Journal* headline is dated September 10, 1928.

Are the people in the photograph of "man standing on car" Mr. Bachechi his family, employees, and a pole sitter? Many believe Mr. Bachechi posed his employees and members of his family for the photograph but Oreste Bachechi died in California on March 12, 1928, at the age of sixty-seven.

Links:

- The KiMo photograph courtesy of the Albuquerque Museum:
  http://www.albuquerquemuseum.org/about/image-licensing

- For more information on the Nicholas P. Ciotola Italians in Albuquerque Pictorial Collection, see
  http://econtent.unm.edu/cdm/landingpage/collection/Ciotola

- For the article on Virginia Doyle, see
  https://www.abqjournal.com/obits/profiles/20225636profiles02-20-10.htm

- For more on the story of Iole Bachechi and Luigi Puccini, see
  http://www.elreyabq.com/history

KiMo Theatre. Circa 1940s.
Courtesy: Albuquerque Museum and KiMo Theatre.

Marquee. *The Man Who Laughs.* Mary Philbin and Conrad Veidt. A silent movie based on an adaptation of Victor Hugo's novel. Circa 1928. Courtesy: Albuquerque Museum and KiMo Theatre.

Marquee. *A Midsummer Night's Dream*. James Cagney and Olivia de Haviland.
Kiva Hi second floor. Circa 1935. Courtesy: KiMo Theatre

The KiMo Theatre, 1920s, and Silent Films

by Brenda Cole

The KiMo Theatre was built as a movie house as well as a great venue for live performances including burlesque. The first silent movie shown was a film entitled *Painting the Town Red*. The first "Talkie" or sound film was the 1929 *Melody of Broadway*. It starred Charles King, Anita Page, Bessie Love and J. Emmett Beck.

The debut of this talking film would have signaled the silencing of the beautiful pipe organ of the theatre. This was also the first sound film to win the Oscar for Best Motion Picture.

Façade. Stagecoach. John Wayne and Claire Trevor. America's Foremost Indian Theatre. Circa 1939.
Courtesy: Albuquerque Museum and KiMo Theatre.

Marquee. *A Midsummer Night's Dream.* Bicycles on Central Avenue.
Circa 1935. Courtesy: KiMo Theatre.

Marquee. Alfred Hitchcock's *Shadow of a Doubt*. Teresa Wright and Joseph Cotton. Kiva Café and Kiva Bar. KGGM radio station sign. Circa 1943.
Courtesy: KiMo Theatre.

KGGM Radio – 1930s

Around this time, the KiMo acquired a new tenant. KGGM radio took over office space on the second floor. They provided a large window so the public could get their first view of how a radio station worked. The station was a CBS affiliate with a program list comprised of soap operas and a bit of news.

Decades later, KGGM became a television station which eventually became known to us as KRQE, Station 13. (The KGGM call sign was reassigned by the FCC in 1994 to an Albuquerque based Christian Music radio station.)

Albuquerque Little Theater

A tenant of another kind came to be associated with the KiMo. The Albuquerque Little Theater began in 1930 and for the first six years of productions called the KiMo home. Many aspiring actors graced the KiMo stage in ALT productions including Vivian Vance, who would later climb to fame as Lucille Ball's sidekick Ethel Mertz.

Recreation in Albuquerque

In the 1920s and 1930s, Central Avenue was a bustling five blocks of commercial activity. Residents shopped and families from farms and ranches came to town to buy supplies. It was a place for adults to gather and share gossip. It was also a meeting place for kids.

During the KiMo's early years, vaudeville acts and other out-of-town road shows brought new and innovative acts to Albuquerque. Some of them sound rather strange to the modern world like; Harvey, the beer drinking bull. One can only imagine what this act involved.

Other names that walked the boards of the old stage were far more well-known: John Carroll, Peter Lind Hayes, Kirk Douglas, Gloria Swanson, Ginger Rogers, Tom Mix, and Mickey Rooney.

There in 1942, Sally Rand performed her famous bubble dance. Most amazing to modern readers would have been the no age restrictions for such a performance.

Central Avenue. Wide shot. Children line Central Avenue.
Circa 1930s. Courtesy: KiMo Theatre.

Central Avenue. America's Foremost Indian Theatre. Enlarged shot.
Children line Central Avenue.
Circa 1930s. Courtesy: KiMo Theatre.

As the years progressed, the KiMo became one of the places to go after school, on the weekends, and when adults or teenagers were craving late night entertainment.

Route 66

In 1937, the "Mother Road" Route 66, ran from North to South through Albuquerque and was part of Fourth Street. After 1937, the Route was moved to follow an East to West direction down Central Avenue, taking it through the heart of the city. The KiMo sits on the northwest corner of Fifth Street and Central Avenue. This brought those traveling across the west on Route 66 right past the front door of the theatre!

The realigning and paving of Route 66 along Central Avenue attracted more tourists to the downtown area. Albuquerque's economic progress brought change to the KiMo. Photos from this era can be seen in the KiMo Theatre ticket office lobby.

1940's Entertainment

During the 1940's, there were several theatres downtown. The Past Time had been renamed The Chief Theatre and showed mainly first-run movies as did the KiMo. At one time, there were as many as four shows a day on Saturdays. There was a children's movie early in the morning, a matinee, the evening performance and then a midnight show as well.

KiMo Theatre façade. *Tropic Holiday*. Dorothy Lamour and Ray Milland. Circa 1938. Courtesy: Albuquerque Museum.

KiMo Theatre. Intersection Central Avenue and Fifth Street. KGGM and CBS sign. Circa 1930s. Courtesy: Albuquerque Museum.

1940's Entertainment

During the 1940's, there were several theatres downtown. The Past Time had been renamed The Chief Theatre and showed mainly first-run movies as did the KiMo. At one time, there were as many as four shows a day on Saturdays. There was a children's movie early in the morning, a matinee, the evening performance and then a midnight show as well.

KiMo Theatre façade. *Tropic Holiday*. Dorothy Lamour and Ray Milland. Circa 1938. Courtesy: Albuquerque Museum.

KiMo Theatre. Intersection Central Avenue and Fifth Street. KGGM and CBS sign. Circa 1930s. Courtesy: Albuquerque Museum.

Competition for the KiMo

by Jacqueline Murray Loring

The Sunshine Theatre, Albuquerque's first movie theatre with over 900 seats, was built in 1924. It stopped showing first-run movies in 1974 and closed completely in the 1980s, but was remodeled and reopened. In 1985, it was named to the National Register of Historic Places.

The KiMo and the Sunshine weren't the only theatres in Albuquerque, nor the only ones on Central Avenue. In its early days, the KiMo Theatre was located at 423 Central Avenue, and shared a one mile stretch of the street with the Rio Theatre, the Sunshine Theatre, and the Pastime*. The El Rey Theatre at 622 Central Avenue was built in 1941, and the State Theatre, which opened in 1949, was located at 225 Central Avenue.

[*Editor's note: Occasionally, the Pasttime Theatre is referred to as the Passtime Theatre or spelled Pass Time]

Playbills and Theatre Memorabilia

The Howard E. Roosa Papers (1925-1947) at the University of New Mexico Center for Southwest Research is a treasure trove of New Mexico theatre memorabilia including playbills from productions at the KiMo Theatre, performed by the Albuquerque Little Theatre Land directed by Kathryn Kennedy O'Connor.

https://rmoa.unm.edu/docviewer.php?docId=nmu1mss227bc.xml

Shopping Malls and Movie Houses

The popularity of the KiMo continued throughout the 1950's with movies and live stage performances, but huge changes were in store for the theatre and the rest of downtown. In the early 1960's a fire almost destroyed the stage and damaged a large section at the front of the house.

Albuquerque's growing population began moving away from the heart of the city. Shopping malls began to replace the individual stores along Central and with them came new multi-screen movie houses with easily accessible parking lots. By 1977, the KiMo Theatre was slated for demolition. The building was saved when the citizens of Albuquerque approved a bond to purchase the theatre. Two major restorations have brought the theatre back to its former glory.

References:
- The Theatre celebrates its 80th Anniversary 26/edhttp://www.abqtrib.com/news/2007/oct/01/albuquerques-kimo-theatre-celebrates- its80th-anni/-1/seq-10/
- Library Thing Local http://www.librarything.com/venue/85279/KiMo-Theatre
- A Virtual tour of the KiMo Theatre http://www.virtualalbuquerque.com/VirtualABQ/KimoTheatre/
- City of Albuquerque KiMo Theatre, Mary McKinney transcript http://www.allreadable.com/2375AF44

Growth and Change in Albuquerque

by Jacqueline Murray Loring

According to Larry Parker, the current manager of the KiMo, "By the time you get into the early 1940s and the end of World War II, vaudeville is basically dead because in ten years talking movies has killed it. Burlesque still stayed in the form of raunchier entertainment but moved to bars and clubs. By the time you get to the mid-1950s, television has killed everything. If you look at the history of the KiMo by timelines, you can understand its rise to the pinnacle of local entertainment and its subsequent fall from grace as new forms of entertainment took its place."

Writer and SouthWest Writers member Kathy Wagoner said, "When Prohibition ended in 1933, visitors and residents no longer needed to use the speakeasy in one of the KiMo's upper rooms. Silent movies gave way to talkies, and new movie stars soon performed on stage. The realigning (and paving) of Route 66 along Central Avenue brought more tourists to downtown Albuquerque in the mid-1930s.

The KiMo had only one competitor, the Sunshine Theater, when it first opened. By 1941, six more theaters were drawing customers away. But Albuquerque's population grew in the 1940s thanks to a few key entities, including: Kirtland Army Air Field, Sandia Base, and Los Alamos National Laboratory's Z Division (later renamed Sandia Laboratory)."

After World War II ended in 1945, East Coasters migrated west. Merchandise stores and restaurants along Central Avenue flourished as both the population of Albuquerque and the University of New Mexico's enrollment increased. Entertainment in Albuquerque was diverse and included an Elvis Presley concert, an evening with Tommy Dorsey, and music by Patsy Cline. (Sadly, none of them at the KiMo.) As abundant as the 1950s were for Albuquerque, the 1960s were the reverse.

Former KiMo Manager Rush Dudley said, "Downtowns across the country were abandoned as people moved to the suburbs in the 1960s. For Albuquerque, in the 1960s, Interstates 40 and 25 divided the city into four quadrants. As people moved to the suburbs they started living within their quadrant, each with their own shopping malls. Those four parts started growing, dividing people.

"Throughout the 1960s and the 1970s, the KiMo was never abandoned. The Bachechi family would show a movie to try to revive Downtown or have performers. But it was never shut down." Dudley concluded, "Thank God for the family and Mrs. Bachechi. Other historic buildings like the Alvarado next to the railroad and the Franciscan Hotel were torn down. Lost forever."

As of the late 1960s, the population of Albuquerque increased but the city needed to spread out. The city could not expand further north because the land was privately owned by the Sandia Pueblo, nor to the south because of Kirtland Air Force Base and the Isleta Pueblo. The Sandia Mountains are east of downtown. As the town spread east and west, core Central Avenue businesses moved east. Other small and large businesses naturally followed and brought a slow decline to the downtown, as well as the KiMo.

Central Avenue. Looking east toward the Sandia Mountain Circa 1950s. Courtesy: Albuquerque Museum and KiMo Theatre

According to Kathy Wagoner, "As the population of Albuquerque increased and spread out, businesses naturally followed and brought a slow decline to the downtown area, as well as the KiMo. Winrock Shopping center was completed in 1961. It was New Mexico's first covered shopping center and included a freestanding movie theater. Coronado Center opened four years later. Progress also answered the population's demand for accessible entertainment, and by 1964 Albuquerque had 11 drive-in theaters in the city. With a steady loss of business and a fire that nearly destroyed the original stage and other areas of the KiMo Theatre in 1963, the KiMo fell into disrepair. By the Mid-1970s, the theatre was slated for destruction."

The City Saves the KiMo

In the 1960s and early 1970s, the KiMo building was owned by the Bachechi Trust, which leased the building to at least one national movie chain, including Commonwealth Theatres. By the mid-1970s, with the combined forces of suburban growth and competition from other theatres and drive-ins, the KiMo fell into decline and disrepair. Like the Alvarado Hotel, the KiMo was slated for destruction.

"The City Attorney, Pat Bryan, went to Mayor David Rusk to encourage the city to buy the KiMo," Parker noted.

In 1977, the citizens of Albuquerque voted to purchase, restore, and preserve the unique and iconic building. One reason often promoted by newspaper reports, published articles, and public opinion for the decision to acquire the KiMo Theatre was the 1970 razing of the Fred Harvey-Alvarado Hotel, which stood several blocks east of the KiMo. It was lost to locals, tourists, and historians.

Author and historian Rudy Miera recalls, "The KiMo was open for live productions after the city bought it. Between 1977 and 1982, I believe it closed the early part of 1982 for renovations, but I think only the orchestra seating was in use. I'm quite sure the balcony was closed."

According to KiMo manager Larry Parker, "In the 1970s before the city bought the KiMo, it was a mixed-use venue. For the city to sustain it after 1977, the structure needed to be available for the community to use. As the old mission seemed to be to make a profit, the new mission was to make the KiMo affordable for the community to use as a rental space for dance, music, theatre, and performing arts."

Watermelon Mountain Jug Band. Left to right: Patrick Houlihan (jug / guitar); Gary Oleson (washtub bass); Barbara Piper (washboard); Ben Perea (banjo /guitar). Circa 2016. Courtesy: Barbara Piper. Photo credit: Shawna Cory.

KiMo Theatre's Jug Band Alley

by Jug Band performer Barbara Piper

Barbara Piper, who plays washboard and percussion and provides background vocals for the band, is a teacher who found music to be an additional passion in life. She is an original member of the Watermelon Mountain Jug Band.

Among the interesting photographs that hang in the KiMo is a picture of Ben Perea, myself, Gary Oleson, Steve Wilkes, and Jeff Burrows taken during a performance by the Watermelon Mountain Jug Band during the 1977 reopening of the KiMo.

The Watermelon Mountain Jug Band is *"one of New Mexico's most treasured natural resources,"* featured in *Fodor's Travel Guide to New Mexico*, named one of *Albuquerque's Legendary Locals* (*Legendary Locals of Albuquerque* by Richard Melzer. UNM Press. 2015), and has performed continuously for forty-three years.

In 1977 (or thereabouts) the KiMo Theatre was reopened with a gala evening of musical entertainment by the band's original members: Gary Oleson, Steve Wilkes, Mark Zimmer, Jeff Burrows, and me. The week the KiMo reopened, we spent our daytime fixing plumbing, scraping gum off the seats, and getting the KiMo spruced up for the evening's performance. Illuminated by spotlights on Central Avenue, the band arrived in a limo in formal attire (yup! The guys wore tuxedos!)

Mayor Harry Kinney honored the band by dedicating the alley behind the KiMo as "Jug Band Alley." That street sign was stolen within two years… And NOT by any band members! But the honor remains.

In 2018, we continue to "play all over town," as our theme song says. Today the band is comprised of Gary Oleson (original member), Barbara Piper (original member), Ben Perea (member for 39 years and the 5-time NM Banjo Champion), and Patrick Houlihan (member for 18 years). The band is still "one of NM's most treasured natural resources." Come see us perform and you'll know why!"

http://www.watermelonmountainjugband.com/

Restoration and Renovation After 1977

By KiMo Manager Rush Dudley

In 1977, after the city bought the KiMo, when the building was reopened, they needed a certificate of occupancy and it was not easy to get one for an older building. There were compromises needed to reopen it. The city had to decide what to do. The mayor's office met with groups including the fire department, building code department, street safety people, disability advocates, and the city attorney. The building was opened, but with some exemptions agreed to by some smart people. They were able to invite the public back into the building but the balcony access was put on hold. During the 1970s, our downtown was literally abandoned but the (Bachechi) family kept trying to keep the KiMo going. The KiMo still showed films.

Thank God the Bachechi family still owned the building because it was scheduled to be torn down as part of urban renewal in the 1970s, and people who knew about it got together and went to City Hall as a citizens committee and said 'we can't lose another historic building!'.

Somehow, they got a grant to purchase and open the building. The mayor at that time, I think it was Dave Rusk, gave the keys to the KiMo to Alan Clarke. Alan Clarke was hired from the New York City library system to build our library. At the time the Albuquerque Library Staff was mostly volunteer. (Mayor David) Rusk told Clarke the city had never owned a theatre and no one had ever worked in one. Rusk told Clarke to "go do something." So, he gave the keys to the KiMo to the director of the library system. Alan Clarke put together a team that included Marge Neset, Tony Marsh, Lauren Griego, and many others.

Alan brought the KiMo up to city codes and the team started booking acts. When you book an act for a theatre, you have to give them a guarantee. You had to write them a check. The West is a hard place to book acts. Acts would do two nights in Kansas City, three nights in Amarillo. Drive to here. Hit Albuquerque for two nights, then on to Phoenix and the West Coast. So, you have to have a guarantee of money ahead of time. The mayor and the city attorney, really, really liked the KiMo, so they sent some money over to book acts.

In the 1980s and 1990s, we booked in acts like Perla Batalla, Pat Graney Company, Don McLean, and the melodrama *1000 Airplanes on the Roof* by Philip Glass. Music producers booked musician George Thorogood and flute player Paul Horn. They brought in jazz performer David Amram. He is one of the saints of jazz. Independent producers booked acts like Taj Mahal, La Zarzuela de Albuquerque, Alex DeGrassi, and Ballet Folklorico Quetzalli.

In 1978, 1979, 1980, after the city bought the KiMo, money was spent to fix part of the stage, the equipment, basic lighting system but they did not restore the entire stage. When it opened, the newly renovated KiMo didn't have experienced technical people to run the theatre for performances. I think I remember Sally Opel from the Opera got a grant and brought in tech people and we helped to trained them to work with other groups. I think Harry Kinney was mayor.

For the KiMo's celebration in 1978, two of the Bachechi sons came to the KiMo and I talked to them. They talked about working for the movie 'fright nights.' They would show monster movies late at night. When World War II ended, there was a party downtown and in the KiMo. The streets filled and the KiMo filled with wall-to-wall people. It was hard to move around because of all the celebrating people.

In the late 1980s and 1990s, performance centers and movie houses saw a drop in attendance as gaming became popular. With limited free cash, many people chose to gamble rather than attend live performances such as opera and ballet. But at the KiMo, theatre prospered.

During the 1980s, the KiMo produced original stage plays and booked performers including Shields and Yarnell, the Blind Boys of Alabama, Doc Watson, and Bill Monroe. The *Underground Nutcracker* was one of the plays produced in the 1980s at the KiMo. It was underwritten by Larry Rainosek, who owns the popular Frontier Restaurant on Central Avenue across from the university. The *Underground Nutcracker* played to full houses.

KiMo Theatre. "Thank You Albuquerque For Saving the KiMo." Circa 1970s. Courtesy: KiMo Theatre.

Links:

- Albuquerque Museum: http://www.albuquerquemuseum.org
- New Mexico Post Alliance: http://newmexicopostalliance.org/
- For more information about the Wurlitzer organ, go to:
  https://www.cabq.gov/culturalservices/kimo/about-the-theatre/kimohistory/pipeorgan
- For more information about the KiMo's restoration, see:
- https://www.cabq.gov/culturalservices/kimo/about-the-theatre/restoration
  For more information on the Carl Von Hassler murals, see
- https://www.cabq.gov/culturalservices/kimo/about-the-theatre/theatre-photos/carl-von- hassler-the-seven-cities-of-cibola-mural-photos

The KiMo and Me: Protecting the KiMo Theatre

By former Albuquerque Mayor David Rusk

Dave Rusk is a former federal official, New Mexico legislator (1975-1977), and mayor of Albuquerque (1977-1981). Since 1993, Rusk has been an independent consultant on urban and suburban policy.
https://www.wilsoncenter.org/book/cities-without-suburbs-census-2010-perspective.

"Mayor?" There was a knock on my open door. "Yes, come in, Alan."

Alan Clarke, Cultural Services Department Director, entered my office on the 8th floor of the old City Hall.

"You know that we've completed buying the KiMo from Commonwealth Theatres?" (At the time, Commonwealth Theatres owned every movie house in Albuquerque.)

"Yes. Congratulations."

"Well, Commonwealth had their administrative offices in that bank of small rooms on the second and third floors facing Central Avenue. They were supposed to clear everything out before the City took over but they missed some filing cabinets. You'll never guess what we found left behind."

"What?"

Alan arched a knowing eyebrow. "Some confidential internal memos describing how Commonwealth bought up all the downtown movie theatres in order to just run them down and close them in order to boost attendance at their more profitable, new multiplexes in the Heights. The KiMo, the State Theatre, the Sunshine—they didn't just die from natural causes. They were murdered."

That was my first experience with the KiMo. City voters had approved a $324,000 bond issue to buy the historic theatre in October 1977—the same election in which I was elected as Albuquerque's second mayor.

Revitalizing Downtown Albuquerque

The very week that I took office, McClellan's Five & Dime, the downtown's last remaining national chain store closed. A recent survey had reported that a quarter of Albuquerque's residents came Downtown only once or twice a year (generally to see the IRS or a judge), and another quarter had *never* come Downtown.

Downtown was pronounced dead.

* * *

During the mayoral campaign, I had described Albuquerque to some audiences as "a giant suburb in search of a city," and Downtown was the only locale that could offer a more urban—and urbane—environment. I announced that Downtown revitalization would be one of my six priorities as mayor.

Downtown would never regain its role as the city's retail trade center. The 1960s-style urban renewal had reinforced Downtown as the federal, state, city, and county government center and the locus of major law offices. It still contained the headquarters site of PNM (the Gas and Electric utility company),

Mountain Bell, several local banks and savings & loans; and the new Albuquerque Convention Center, but these produced a very sterile, 9-to-5 environment.

I thought that Downtown could become the region's arts and entertainment center, converting many of the vacant storefronts and second- and third-story rooms into art galleries and artists' lofts as home to what I knew was a very vigorous local contemporary arts scene (more so than Santa Fe).

As a renovated performing arts center, the KiMo Theatre would be the centerpiece of that transformation. So I rejected the conventional wisdom that "people won't come Downtown." They'll come Downtown if we give them something really exciting to come Downtown to, I decreed.

Downtown Saturday Night

So in its unrenovated, quasi-abandoned state, the KiMo's first use was as the office space from which Alan Clarke, Marge Neset, and a cadre of enthusiastic volunteers organized a 13-week series of Downtown Saturday Nights which were set up on a closed-off Central Avenue and Fourth Street, Albuquerque's historic crossroads. (I had to overcome initial staff preferences for the Civic Plaza, still today a soul less, forbidding, concrete wasteland, and demand genuine street festivals on Central Avenue.)

Of course, the series included Hispanic Heritage Night, Black Culture Night, Native American Night, but my real thrust was to disaggregate that catchall term "Anglo" to unveil the tremendous diversity that is Albuquerque's reality. So, we had (as I recall) A Night in Paris (sponsored by the Alliance Française), Saxons, Celts, and Vikings Night (British, Irish, and Scandinavians), Slavic Night (Poles and other Eastern Europeans), Japanese

Night, Mediterranean Night (Italians, Greeks, and Turks), Oktoberfest in August (German-American Society), a Country Western Night (a nod to our frontier culture), and several others.

Each featured the ethnic foods of the sponsoring groups, traditional songs and dances presented on a temporary stage at 4th and Central Avenue, ethnic costumes, traditional games, etc., and beer flowing under the tolerant eyes of the Albuquerque Police Department (APD) officers. Some national societies were organized *for the first time ever* in order to sponsor their Downtown Saturday Night. Most surviving Central Avenue businesses remained open for Downtown Saturday Night or hawked their wares/food from tables in front of their establishments.

The people loved it.

APD estimated that Downtown Saturday Night attracted 30,000-40,000, a night that packed Central Avenue and side streets from 2nd to 6th. Even those city councilors who had been critical of how I had pooled together about $300,000 from different departmental budgets enjoyed coming down.

Among Albuquerqueans who didn't love Downtown Saturday Night were two ultraconservative Republican ladies who were literally the stereotypical "little old ladies with purple hair in tennis shoes." The "two Dorothys" (as I dubbed them) launched a Recall Mayor Rusk petition drive—one of four abortive efforts to recall me—over Downtown Saturday Night and other supposed examples of my "spendthrift," fiscally irresponsible ways.

In any event, though probably thirty years ahead of its time, Downtown Saturday Night heralded Downtown's potential as Albuquerque's premier entertainment zone—and it was all planned out of the KiMo's office on the corner of Fifth and Central Avenue.

Planning the KiMo's Renovation

During that very summer, the KiMo held its first public function. Knowing my love for the KiMo, Police Chief Bob Stover decided to hold graduation ceremonies for the latest Police Academy class in the KiMo. His daughter emailed me recently about that ceremony being her own first memory of the KiMo as a little girl.

So, 11 a.m. on an unwontedly humid August weekday found a couple of dozen cadets, Chief Stover, myself, and other city dignitaries up on the narrow stage while proud family and friends filled the first rows of the dimly lit, dusty auditorium.

I remember little of the ceremony itself except that the ancient air-conditioning system didn't work, the holdover old arc lights blazed down on the stage, and as I sat there in my business suit, sweat began to impregnate my clothes. I had never been so hot and uncomfortable in any indoors locale in my life. I realized that the recently acquired KiMo would be totally unusable unless it underwent substantial renovation and modernization.

So, the Cultural Affairs Department engaged local architect Harvey Hoshour to lay out a thorough renovation and expansion of the KiMo. Harvey developed about a $2-2.5 million plan that would completely redo the auditorium (though restoring all the historic decorations of "America's Premier Indian Theatre"), create new lobby/gallery space and restrooms in the storefront next door, and ultimately extend the KiMo to include a small auditorium for smaller productions in the storefront long occupied by the funky, iconic Freed's store. (The Freed family resisted the City's buying the property; an option was ultimately negotiated in which the property would be acquired by the City only after the death of Max Freed, but although Max Freed has long since passed on, four decades later, Freed's is still there.)

Well over half the cost would be provided by a grant from the Federal Economic Development Administration. I had secured the Federal grant commitment (to be matched by city bond funds) through the Carter White House. About a $1 million standalone local bond issue was placed on the October 1979 bond election as matching funds to renovate the KiMo.

But in the years leading up to this election the political climate had changed. To constant coverage from the national press, angry voters in California enacted Proposition 13, which capped local property taxes at a crippling level. Former California Governor Ronald Reagan was gearing up his challenge to Jimmy Carter the next year. Conservatives were pounding the drumbeat that "Americans are overtaxed ... Americans are overtaxed ... cut taxes ... cut taxes," despite the objective fact that then (and now) Americans pay the third- or fourth-lowest total tax rate of any advanced, free-market society!

The bond issue to renovate the KiMo was defeated, though street bonds, library bonds, etc. passed (with lower than traditional margins).

The Dilemma

So, I was left with a dilemma. On the one hand, city voters had approved using taxpayer money to buy the KiMo as a "performing arts center." On the other hand, city voters had rejected using taxpayer money to fix it up so that it could actually be used as a performing arts center or for anything at all. Plus, in the wake of the failed bond election, the City lost the $1.5 million federal matching grant.

So, what to do? We sent Harvey Hoshour back to the drawing board to come up with a minimal plan for making the KiMo at least usable for the performing arts. After a number of months Harvey proposed a minimal plan: upgrade the electric systems (including new HVAC); new seating downstairs (but not in the balcony); essential lobby space and restrooms to meet modern code requirements; a modest orchestra pit; and new stage and lighting equipment for theatrical productions. Price tag: $1.1 million. With the support of a majority of the City Council, I pulled together $1.1 million from various departmental budgets to fund the minimal renovation process, but I paid a big political price. Talk radio rang with denunciations of how Mayor Rusk had "defied the voters" by moving forward with the KiMo. That may have been a key factor in my losing campaign for reelection, as I was narrowly squeezed out of the runoff, coming in third in a ten-candidate field in October 1981.

The KiMo's Greatest Nights

As my term ended in December 1981, the KiMo's actual renovation had not yet begun. But I was hovering nearby both literally as a PNM (Public Service Company of New Mexico) corporate executive at its Alvarado Square Downtown headquarters and spiritually as board member, chief fundraiser, and chorus member of the Albuquerque Opera Theatre (AOT).

My dream was to move AOT from UNM's (University of New Mexico) Popejoy Hall (which was overlarge for our productions and audience) into the KiMo as its resident company for three to five productions a year. As renovation proceeded, worried that cost overruns might cancel out the orchestra pit (essential for the opera company), I constantly checked on progress with Alan Clarke.

The Great Night finally arrived. In the fall of 1982 (I believe), the KiMo opened with AOT's production of Puccini's *Tosca* on a Friday and Sunday night. With other male chorus members, I donned my costume and greasepaint in the very barebones, cramped male dressing room next to the women's dressing room under the KiMo's stage. (The stars readied themselves in unrenovated smaller rooms off the theatre's stage left stairwell.)

Under guest conductor John Landis, the orchestra struck up the opening chords. The curtain pulled back. Dimly illuminated by the stage lights, the faces of 700-plus ticket holders faded into the shadows of the orchestra seating and the far recesses of the overhanging balcony.

A Packed House

After the first act's opening scene, the chorus was finished. I disappeared into the dressing room again, wiped off my greasepaint, and climbed back into civilian clothes. By the beginning of the second act, I was standing in the back of the balcony, watching my dream unfold. The audience was so wrapped up in watching Tosca dispatch the evil Baron Scarpia that I'm sure nobody even noticed me standing there. The acoustics were excellent. The onstage action seemed intimately close. It was perfect.

Over the next nine years, I sang in the chorus, hustled season ticket renewals (I would call every season ticket holder personally), and struggled to raise business community donations to finance AOT's productions—*Rigoletto*, *Carmen*, *Faust*, *The Merry Wives of Windsor*, *Die Fledermaus*, *La Bohème*, *Madame Butterfly*—they went on and on. And I think they helped provide a second life for the KiMo greater than its first life.

Reflections

In 1991, we moved from Albuquerque back to Washington, D.C. By the mid-2000s, I had completely lost my hearing and could no longer follow the opera world. And of course, from a distance of 1,800 miles, I could no longer attend the KiMo.

But every time we visit Albuquerque, I make a point of systematically walking Downtown from Coal to Lomas, 1st to 8th to see what's new—both the good (all the bars and restaurants, the multiscreen movie complex, the hundreds of new apartments) and the bad (the emptying out of south of Central Avenue office space as federal offices have shifted to the new Pete V. Domenici United States Courthouse on Lomas, plus PNM's vacant Alvarado Square). And I always duck into the KiMo office to greet the city staff (for whom I am only, at best, a vaguely remembered name) and to ask for a special chance to reenter the auditorium and visit old backstage haunts.

Some folks remember me as "the mayor who saved the KiMo." That's not really true. It was Mayor Harry Kinney, Albuquerque's historic preservationists, and 1977 bond issue voters who saved the KiMo from demolition. But I helped the KiMo be reborn. And I count that as one of my life's greatest professional achievements."

For more information: https://vimeo.com/57236969

KiMo Theatre Grand Reopening

Text of Media Release.

Nuevo Mexico, Si!

A Musical Drama of the State's History presented by La Compañía de Teatro de Alburquerque.

The public is invited to dress in a historical costume (optional) and join Lieutenant Governor Robert Mondragón and La Compañía at 6:30PM for a procession from San Felipe de Neri Church in Old Town to the KiMo where Archbishop Roberto Sanchez will bless the building and cast. Mariachi and Infanteria Colonial Alburquerque will participate in the procession. KiMo Theatre, Fifth and Central Avenue. Saturday, September 11, 1982. Festivities begin at 7:30PM.

Information. Courtesy: Rudy Miera

The Grand Reopening 1982

by Rudy J. Miera

Rudy J. Miera was a teacher for over twenty years and a member of La Compañía de Teatro de Alburquerque. He acted in Nuevo Mexico, Sí! and played guitar for La Compañía's plays. For a while, he, along with Rebeca Benjamin and other educators, worked as coordinators between the school systems and La Compañía, ensuring attendance of students for the shows at the KiMo.

A Home for Performing Artists

For five straight days, from September 8 to September 12, 1982, New Mexicans, tourists, and visitors alike celebrated the reopening of the KiMo Theatre as a home for live theatre, dance, music, and of course, movies. One flyer from the 1982 KiMo Theatre Grand Reopening announces: KiMo GRAND OPENING featuring *"Nuevo Mexico, Sí!"*

Nuevo Mexico, Sí! was the centerpiece of La Compañía de Teatro de Alburquerque long-running repertory. The original musical, written for and performed by La Compañía continuously for over a year, depicted the history of New Mexico from the Anasazi to modern times. It was written by José

Rodriguez, one of La Compañía's cofounders, who taught workshops at the University of Albuquerque (previously the College of St. Joseph). The plays that emerged from these workshops resulted in two productions (including *Bodas de Sangre* by Federico García Lorca) and the formation of La Compañía de Teatro de Alburquerque. Patrice Martinez, lead stage actress for La Compañía which was cofounded by her mother, Margarita Martinez, went on to play opposite Steve Martin, Chevy Chase, and Martin Short in the film *Three Amigos!*

Nuevo Mexico, Sí!

José Rodriguez was a resident artist for La Compañía de Teatro de Alburquerque, Premier Bilingual Theatre Company. He was an ex-priest who started a bilingual company. He brought classic plays from Spain and produced them in English and Spanish which brought South Valley people and the North Valley people back to the KiMo. The great jazz workshops would bring students and teachers from the University.

From 1977 to the renovation was a time of trying to bring folks back Downtown. The view then was that Downtown was abandoned and unsafe. We fought back that perception. What happened was people returned Downtown. Those shows often sold out. Because people came back Downtown, the city used that fact to get that first funding for renovations, which was a federal grant.

Photos Above scanned from the

La Compañía Flyer. *Sí, Hay Posada.*
Directed by Irene Olever Lewis. Courtesy: Rudy Miera.

The city could justify asking for federal money because audiences came. It was one of the last federal grants for building restorations because Ronald Reagan became president. So, the money showed up. The first renovations focused on safety on the front of the house*, and they did a little work on the stage.

The dedication written on the flyer for the 1980 *Sí, Hay Posada* Christmas play reads: "José Rodriguez's achievement as a teacher and spiritual leader can be seen in every aspect of La Compañía's work. It is to José that we fondly dedicate this production. Bienvenidos, Jose!"

After staging a couple of productions at the old University of Albuquerque, the group that became La Compañía de Teatro de Albuquerque found a welcoming home at the KiMo Theatre. In late 1979, *El Sueño del Santero* was presented at the theatre in the heart of Downtown Albuquerque at 5th and Central Avenue. The success of having community members from Duranes to San José, from Old Town to Los Griegos neighborhoods in attendance led to several seasons of live theatre at the KiMo prior to the eventual residence at Nuestro Teatro in the Nob Hill area.

La Compañía Finds Temporary *posada*** at the KiMo.

[*Editor's note: The front of the house includes the main curtain, audience area, lobby, front of building, and outside.]
[**Editor's note: dwelling, shelter]

La Compañía had a core group of actors but no dedicated technicians at the time. The Artistic Director was Margarita Martinez, assistant to José. They established a fruitful artistic relationship with the KiMo staff. We used technicians for sound and lighting who worked for the KiMo. Rush Dudley helped with lighting constructions and E. Harlughe Flejtuchovich was our audio consultant. The KiMo collaborated with us, allowed us to rehearse on their stage and helped with publicity and the box office. In 1980, the KiMo opened up and supported an entirely new movement of community theatre."

Sí, Hay Posada 1980

Using the original folk play of *Las Posadas*, brought to North America by the Spaniards several centuries ago, Denise Chavez used the story of Joseph and Mary's journey to Bethlehem and their search for a place to stay as a play-within-a-play and the jumping-off point for her script of *Sí, Hay Posada*. (Staging of *Las Posadas* has been a cultural tradition in New Mexico since the mid-17th century.)

Directed by Irene Oliver-Lewis (Denise's cousin) for the 1980 Christmas season on the KiMo stage, the bilingual production, funded by the New Mexico Arts Division, played to enthusiastic crowds that came from all areas of the city. The contemporary retelling had a large cast, featuring Margo Chavez-Charles (Denise's sister), the late, beloved actress Angie Torrez, Mark Kilburn, Rudy J. Miera (as Tito Terrazas), and Indigenous music by Ayocuan.

The KiMo Folklore

Most stage actors are used to observing and respecting certain rituals, like encouraging eachother to "break a leg" before a performance, never mentioning the name *Macbeth* in a theatre, instead referring to "the Scottish play," and like leaving a bare light bulb on all night on the center of the main stage.

One theatrical tradition gives homage to a ghost or two that may be trapped in the theatre. In the cast of the KiMo, the long-time ghost is that of a boy, Bobby, who was said to have died when a hot-water pipe in the theatre burst. Actors are encouraged to leave poems, soft drinks, small toys, or favorite foods to appease the restless spirit(s).

I was introduced to the legend of Bobby during our tech rehearsals at the KiMo. If I remember correctly, before our full house performance of *Nuevo Mexico, Sí!*, I left him part of a stale doughnut, which remained untouched for weeks. I wonder how long it stayed in that small backstage shrine …

Although this experience was my first introduction to the ghost of the KiMo, in the end, it is the stories embodied in the real lives of people like Padre José Martínez and Doña Tules, and fictional characters like Jesús Chavez and Don Quixote, which go on living in the memories of visitors to the KiMo Theatre.

La Compañía de Teatro de Alburquerque

"From Don Juan de Oñate to R.C. Gorman, New Mexico's Multicultural History, Live on the KiMo Theatre Stage" By Rudy J. Miera

"Rudy, I have some good news! The City of Albuquerque has asked La Compañía to do *Nuevo Mexico, Sí!* at the KiMo Theatre in September!" Margarita Martinez, a cofounder of La Compañía de Teatro de Alburquerque, the city's first bilingual repertory theatre company, was sharing the amazing news with me and a couple of the other core actors of the troupe.

"That is great news," I exclaimed. "In fact, it's gonna be historic, *Diós mio*, think of the people who have performed on that famous stage before us, from Judy Garland to Mickey Rooney! You know, when my mom was a kid, growing up in the Barelas neighborhood, they would bring the Ballet Folklorico dancers there, my mom included, after they had perfected their *bailes* on the Barelas Community Center stage."

The grand reopening of the KiMo would be on September 11, and Cultural Affairs personnel from the city wanted everyone dressed in a historical costume. From Lieutenant Governor Roberto Mondragón to Archbishop Roberto Sanchez all marching in a procession to Fifth and Central Avenue. For this night of the festivities there were plans for one of those old Hollywood premiere lights that reach up to the clouds in the night sky.

In fact, the 1982 reopening, after extensive remodeling, ran from September 8 through September 12, and included Native American drama and song, a dance review, jazz musicians, and the Watermelon Mountain Jug Band.

The Cultural Affairs personnel from the city were organizing the weeklong celebration. I was in the first several years of teaching art at the Youth Diagnostic Center, and like the other core actors in the group, I was performing on Friday and Saturday evenings and Sunday afternoons.

Nuevo Mexico, Sí! was a two-act musical drama containing lots of satire of politicians. It gave an abbreviated overview of key historical events, celebrated in songs from "Zuñi Lullaby" to "Oñate's Lament," from the "Army of the West" to Waltz of the Governors."

One of the very most ambitious home-grown productions ever to be mounted on stage in the Duke City, the two-hour plus pageant ran from Fall 1981 for over a year, the 100th performance timed to take place at the KiMo reopening in 1982.

Nuevo Mexico, Sí!, written by José Rodriguez, the other cofounder, was the centerpiece of La Compañía's long-running repertory. Songs and score were composed by Noble Shropshire, who took a leave of absence from a Broadway show. José, was a classically trained Puerto Rican actor and director. He came to Albuquerque to fulfill an invitation from Dr. Miguel Encinias to direct Federico García Lorca's *Bodas de Sangre* (*Blood Wedding*) at the University of Albuquerque and ended up moving here, finding a large, popular audience for Spanish and bilingual theatre. (The template for *Nuevo Mexico, Sí!* was *Puerto Rico, Vá*, also a musical telling of historical characters.)

The idea of softening the process and results of colonization, dramatizing cultural clashes, and honoring cultural exchanges was successfully adapted to the retelling of New Mexico's multicultural past and present.

Come to the KiMo Theatre
Grand Opening

Dance Music, Laughter, Magic, Champagne.

In the Spirit of KiMo – Native American Dance, Drama & Song on September 8. Watermelon Mountain Jug Band – Always a Standing Ovation on September 9.

New Mexico Jazz Workshop – Hari Hamilton & World/ Jess Sawyer and the Prophets/ The William Morris Agency on September 10.

La Compañía de Teatro de Alburquerque "Nuevo Mexico, Sí!" on September 11. New Mexico Dance – A Dance Review on September 12.

1927…Live…At the KiMo…The Cars…The Stars…A Cast of Thousands and You! Tickets Available at All Giants Ticket Outlets. Festivities begin at 7:30 PM.

Adults $5.00 Seniors and Children $3.00.

The text of the second flyer for the same event documents the multicultural, community participation in the reopening:
Flyer. Courtesy: Rudy J. Miera.

Ehecatl Aztec Dancers. Unity poster. Day of the Dead celebration. Circa 1990s.
Courtesy: Rudy Miera. Photo credit: Rudy Miera

Kalpulli Ehecatl

Another group which performed for the Rededication of the KiMo in 1982 were the Kalpulli Ehecatl Aztec Dancers. A recurring KiMo favorite, the Ehecatl Aztec Dancers presented their traditional dance and blessings to the four directions. Kalpulli Ehecatl is a warrior-style dance and musical group based in Albuquerque and founded by Mapitzmitl Xiukwetzpaltzin (PAZ) following the death of mentor Florencio Yescas. PAZ traces his heritage back to the founding families of New Mexico.

According to PAZ, Ehecatl's leader and historian, Ehecatl is primarily a community, family-based group. The family has been performing at events at the KiMo for over 30 years. The first component of Kalpulli Ehecatl is dance. The second component is a series of cultural awareness workshops and lectures. Public performances are a mixture of music, dance, and storytelling and are presented in a tri-lingual format of Nahuatl or Aztec, Spanish, and English.

"We see performing as a means of sharing our dance and culture with our audience, and building relations through cultural sharing." PAZ said.

1982 Grand Reopening Day

On September 11, 1982, theatrical history was made at the KiMo when a musical drama of the history of the state of New Mexico was again performed by La Compañía de Teatro de Alburquerque, who had been presenting *Nuevo Mexico, Si!* since June of 1981.

All 600-plus seats in the renovated KiMo Theatre were filled with audience members, from university students to carpenters, from lawyers to post office deliverymen, from housewives to legislators. (Fortunately for me, my Uncle Pete Miera and his wife, Fay Miera, happened to be visiting from California and were guests of my father and mother.) There were some in the crowd that night who had seen the spirited spectacle previously, but most were anticipating their first glimpse of New Mexico's outstanding movers and shakers, from early Spanish colonist Juan de Oñate to Native American artist R.C. Gorman.

There was a great dance piece in the play called "The Waltz of the Governors" that portrayed the history from 1912 to 1943 in one waltz with the

State symbolized by a woman in a fiesta dress, dancing with one outstanding governor after another.

Historical high points were portrayed all the way up to the atomic bomb being exploded. Thousands of school kids saw this production, intended for all ages. Many performances were sold out days in advance and there was almost always a full house in attendance. On Saturday, September 11, 1982, the lieutenant governor was there, in Albuquerque's Downtown, to join Archbishop Sanchez, who blessed the new building, reestablishing the KiMo as a friendly house for the community to host theatre and performing arts.

Mezzanine railing. *Macbeth* banner.
A KiMo Theatre and Vortex Theatre production.
Circa 2013. Courtesy: Rush Dudley.

The KiMo Theatre History in the New Millennium-2000 to 2017

Renovations Bring KiMo Up to City Codes

by Jacqueline Murray Loring

The KiMo Theatre renovations begun in the late 1990s continued into early 2000. A new stage ceiling, rigging hardware, and stage draperies completed the work. New lobby entry doors into the auditorium were added. Also completed in 2000 was the installation of new seating and carpet, a main stage curtain, new tech booth, lighting positions hidden between and behind vigas (roof beams) on the ceiling and a re-creation of the KiMo's original proscenium arch.

The 1999-2000 renovations were completed just in time for the 2001 celebration of the 75th anniversary of historic Route 66. Over the winter of 2000-2001, the KiMo's second-floor business offices were renovated to meet current building and safety codes. The third-floor office area was renovated in 2002. Work included upgrading plumbing and electrical systems, a new telephone system, and new roofing. The auditorium seating capacity that began with over 1,000 seats in 2017 is just over 650.

Kathy Wagoner said, "With up-to-date lighting, screening, and sound systems, the KiMo serves as an affordable venue for many local groups with calendar dates that can fill up a year in advance. Among the folks and groups who have appeared at the KiMo are the New Mexico Philharmonic, Keshet Dance Company, New Mexico Film Office, and the 48 Hour Film Project, which presents original short films made for their annual competition."

National and International Recording Artists

In the early 2000s, with the renovations complete, the KiMo served as an affordable venue for many local groups with calendar dates that can fill up a year in advance. Concerts at the KiMo included nationally known artists such as Lebanese composer and singer Marcel Khalife; singer and guitarist Greg Brown; traditional Irish instrumental band Lúnasa; songwriter, singer, and poet Rodney Crowell; singers Mavis Staples, Suzanne Vega, and Laurie Anderson; and legendary entertainment figures such as Navajo-Ute flute player R. Carlos Nakai and singers Joan Baez, Arlo Guthrie, and Buffy Sainte-Marie with Shannon McNally. In 2012, concert promoter Joe Anderson presented American musician, writer, singer, actor, spoken word poet, and social commentator Henry Rollins during his *The Long March Tour* at the KiMo.

Two Theatrical Seasons

KiMo manager Larry Parker summarizes the KiMo's performance year this way. "There are two seasons at the KiMo. Labor Day to Memorial Day, which is considered the 'theatrical' season where we do seventy-five to eighty-five percent of our yearly business. We feature the Ballet, the Young Actors, and Opera.

Then there is also Memorial Day to Labor Day season. We keep up with the needs for technology of the new groups. In 2013, the KiMo Theatre went digital, which expanded its opportunity to bring in a wide variety of entertainment and a richer experience for audiences.

Each year, concert promoters including Neal Copperman, executive director of AMP Concerts, and Joe Anderson do a brilliant job of matching of acts and talent to the size of the KiMo. They book performances featuring national and international recording artists. They average about six to eight concerts at the KiMo each year. Anderson is the owner of the Launch Pad in Albuquerque. He presents shows at the KiMo as JAWERKS."

Horror Movies

In the summer of 2014, Parker was interviewed by Anthony DellaFlora on the City of Albuquerque's GOV-TV channel for a program titled *Coming to the KiMo*. According to Parker, "By 2008, the KiMo was primarily a third-party rental venue with approximately sixty percent of its monthly calendar dates filled.

Under the new administration of Mayor Berry, the City of Albuquerque proposed to fill the empty nights with local programing and film-specific nights. Wednesdays featured European foreign films, Thursdays (films) that might feature actors like Marilyn Monroe, and Friday was Fright Night, upholding a long tradition at the KiMo of showing scary movies that featured (actors like) Bela Lugosi and Lon Chaney." For a fun discussion of horror films by Parker and DellaFlora, see the link at the end of this section.

Burlesque is Back

Beginning in 2006, the KiMo added to its yearly lineup Southwest Burlesque, which is restricted to folks eighteen years of age and older. Each performance features dancers, singers, aerialists, and comedians performing a tribute to the art of burlesque and to the olden days of the KiMo.

Classical KiMo

In March 2012, the KiMo presented *Philharmonithon*, an all-day, free event sponsored by Integrated Control Systems. A live broadcast on Classical 95.5 KHFM began at 6 a.m. and continued until 7 p.m. Live entertainment was provided through the courtesy of the New Mexico Philharmonic. The event included a silent auction.

The Philharmonic also presented at the KiMo "An Introduction to the Classics" on Saturday, September 29, 2012. Guest conductor Clark Suttle led the orchestra in a performance of Ludwig van Beethoven's Fifth Symphony. The music and concert series was hosted by Brent Stevens of KHFM.

Another exciting evening at the KiMo for fans of the Philharmonic was a sponsored concert on September 30, 2012: PULSE Performance titled "Changing the World." It included viewing scenes from two films produced and narrated by Albuquerque filmmaker Chris Schueler. New Mexican Jeff Jolly composed the scores for both films. The choir of Albuquerque's New Hope Full Gospel Baptist Church is heard in *Looking In*, and a children's choir from local churches and schools is heard in *The First Millimeter*. In addition, the concert presented a video made by teachers and students of Albuquerque Studios Film & Technology Academy of Atrisco Heritage Academy High School and from

DATA Charter High School. Daniel Davis of Albuquerque composed the music for the video. The Philharmonic performed the music of the films and the video.

Architects and the KiMo

The American Institute of Architects (AIA) Albuquerque invited the community to the KiMo to attend "A Life in Architecture Annual Lecture Series". According to their web site, the September 2013 lecture was part of an annual lecture series "that brings prominent architects to speak about their work and ideas. The lecture series first started when AIA Albuquerque hosted the City of Albuquerque's Tricentennial architecture month in 2005."

Public Art Celebration

On October 10, 2013, the KiMo hosted the official birthday celebration for the Albuquerque Public Art Program's 35th birthday. It was the same day the Urban Enhancement Trust Fund celebrated its 30th birthday. Betty Rivera, Director of Albuquerque's Cultural Services Department, and Dan Mayfield were the masters of ceremonies. The event hosted an exhibition of public artworks displayed in the KiMo Theatre Art Gallery. Local guitarist Harry Irizarry played guitar in the lobby as guests mingled. Formed in 2003, the Fractal Foundation whose mission is to "use the beauty of fractals to inspire interest in science, math and art" presented a fractal slideshow as guests entered the theatre. Albuquerque's inaugural Poet Laureate (2012-2014), Hakim Bellamy, performed an original poem about the Public Art Collection titled "Sidewalk Society" alongside four members of the Tricklock Company. Other performers that day included Chatter; Kahlila Hughes, presented by the Outpost Performance Space; and Sadaqah, presented by the Asian American Association of New Mexico.

An Overview of the Diverse Programing at the KiMo Theatre

Though the KiMo no longer shows first-run movies, it does support the independent and local movie-making industry and features a vibrant series of film retrospectives during certain seasons each year. The theatre can also be reserved for art shows and private events

A quick look of the entertainment and programming offered at the KiMo over the next several years shows diverse content but the KiMo continued to included ballet, opera, and Young Actors' performances. In 2013, the KiMo Theatre in cooperation with the Consulate of Mexico presented a vintage film festival; in July 2014, audiences witnessed the Organization of Competitive Bodybuilders' presentation of "Drug-Free Bodybuilding" and a bikini contest. Each year the schedule continued to include Southwest Burlesque.

More Magic

In 2013, the KiMo introduced for the first time the "Albuquerque Hocus Pocus Magic Show". "It's a great holiday show for all ages," Larry Parker said of the Hocus Pocus. "It has played at the KiMo on Thanksgiving weekend for five years. A family brought it here and it is such a hit, they bring it back from LA each year and open it to the general public. Very popular."

The Magic Show website claims, "Once you step into the lobby you will be transformed into a world where magic rules, and there are no rules!" and "Sophisticated magic, comedy, and unusual acts from around the world." The rundown of magicians who perform at the KiMo are some of the world's "top magicians." "…stars 5 award winning magicians from the Magic Castle in Hollywood."

KiMo lobby, stairways mezzanine, railing, and Carl Von Hassler's murals. Circa 1930's. Courtesy: Albuquerque Museum

KiMo Theatre: Fact and Folklore

SECTION II

The Personal Impact of the Theatre Memories

KiMo Theatre: Fact and Folklore

Memories of Rick Rhodes and Margo Radaelli
KiMo employees from 1977 to 1984

By Dianne R. Layden

Dianne R. Layden is a semi-retired college professor, award-winning writer, and editor of an historical society newsletter in Albuquerque, New Mexico. Her interests include New Mexico history and culture.

As a child, I asked my mother if there is a heaven. She replied that the good things people do on earth live after them. I believed her. KiMo Theatre employee Rick Rhodes left a trail of good memories for his friends when, in December 2008, he passed away at age 64. A particularly nice guy, he was distinctive with his bright blond hair and broad smile. Rick was proudly gay. He and his partner, Barry Soprano, met in New Orleans and were together about twenty years. Barry passed away in 2006.

Rick worked for the KiMo for fifteen years, rising from box office clerk to front-of-house manager to business manager. Cultural Services director Dana Feldman, who was hired in 2009, said she didn't know Rick but heard about him. KiMo manager Larry Parker knew Rick the last months of his life and agreed he was a good representative of the KiMo's employees to feature in an anthology celebrating the KiMo's 90th anniversary.

Margot Radaelli was hired by the KiMo part-time after she completed her degree in theatre at the University of New Mexico (UNM) and worked there in 1977-1984 and 1994-2004. She performed all kinds of jobs, whatever was needed--set designer, stage manager, ticket seller, popcorn-maker, janitor; she also chased pigeons off the roof. She met Rick in 1994 and became a close friend. She said Rick was born in Roswell, NM and served in the military in the Philippines.

My interview with Margot provided interesting details about the KiMo's history. For remodels, Margot researched the Navajo swastikas, the wrought iron railings along the stairways up to the mezzanine, the Carl Von Hassler murals and the meaning of Pueblo Deco designs, such as the cow skulls. The swastikas, which are ancient symbols found worldwide in indigenous cultures, were covered with paper during World War II, due to Nazi Germany's adoption of an adaptation of the symbol.

During one remodel, the wrought iron had to be redone to comply with City code. The turkeys in the railing were symbols of the unknown artist's pueblo when the KiMo was built in 1927. To raise the railings, wrought iron was added to their necks and legs. Visitors often say they look like flamingos and ask about their origin.

Also, the KiMo had a valuable carbon arc film projector on the third floor in a booth lined with lead that only employees could enter. Following a remodel, the projector was placed on display on the mezzanine.

Mezzanine landing with railing and Carl Von Hassler' murals. Circa 1930s. Courtesy: Albuquerque Museum.

Rick Rhodes was also a graphic artist who printed his work at the Tamarind Institute near UNM and at the New Grounds Print Workshop in Nob Hill. He and Margot, who creates religious folk art, travelled together to Europe several times and to art exhibits in American cities. On his own, Rick visited Egypt four times. Margo noted that Rick volunteered once a week for over twenty years as a dishwasher at Project Share on Yale SE, where she herself volunteered for nine years. She described him as "so positive."

Margot referred to herself and Rick as soulmates. She cared for him for four months when he was ill, staying at his house and taking him to medical appointments, including radiation treatments. They spoke of growing old together and sharing his house, which had two rooms that would serve as studios for both of them. This wasn't to be. On Christmas morning of 2008,

Margot found Rick on the floor of his home. He had passed away.

I knew Rick from our encounters both at the KiMo and the Unitarian Universalist Fellowship. In 2004-2010, in addition to teaching at Central New Mexico Community College, I was an academic advisor at a private university that held its graduations at the KiMo. Rick was a longtime member of the UU (First Unitarian Church of Albuquerque) Fellowship, which meets at the Albuquerque Peace and Justice Center near UNM.

I remember when Rick told the Fellowship he had cancer, and when we were told Rick passed away. I felt as if a friend I was just getting to know was torn away from me. His many friends held a memorial service, which I attended.

Fellowship members Bill Riker and his wife, Christy, knew Rick and Barry well. Bill and Christy began vacationing in New Mexico in the mid-1990s and stayed at their bed-and-breakfast north of Old Town. The partners later split up. Bill remembers Rick as "down-to-earth with a great sense of humor and engaging laugh." Rick retired from the KiMo early after he learned he had cancer, and for Bill his passing so soon after retirement was heart-rending.

From several people I interviewed, as well as my own brief acquaintance, I learned Rick Rhodes truly served his community and delighted his many friends who loved him.

[Editor's note: For more information about the KiMo Theatre's architecture, see Section III. The Tour of the KiMo Theatre.]

A Paranormal Place

by Jacqueline Murray Loring

Whether fact, fiction, opinion, or folklore, the KiMo has been called by some "the best-known haunted theatre in the Land of Enchantment," maybe the entire American Southwest.

In 1951, the folklore about a ghost at the KiMo began with the tragic explosion of a water heater. The story goes that the boiler (or water pipe) exploded at the exact time a boy was either on his way downstairs from the balcony to buy treats at the concession stand, or left the balcony after becoming frightened by the movie he was watching with young friends, or was walking downstairs from the mezzanine to leave the theatre. What is fact and where does folklore begin?

The little boy's name often changes with reports of the tragedy from Bobby Darnall to Bobby Parnell. Fact is: the front page of the next morning's newspaper reported the explosion and the boy's death. But what about the paranormal part of the story? Skeptics refute the existence of Bobby's ghost, and his family might consider it disrespectful to talk about nonproven stories, but the accident did happen and a child's life was tragically lost.

Over the years, performers at the KiMo, not wanting to test the folklore or annoy a ghost if there were one, began to bring tributes for Bobby, and a backstage shrine evolved in his honor. KiMo performers continue into 2018 to bring trinkets to the shrine. Some performers say they take a moment before going onstage to stand at the shrine and take a deep breath to focus.

Doubters notwithstanding, people report seeing the six-year-old playing on the lobby staircase or looking out an upstairs window. And then there is the story about a lady in a bonnet walking the KiMo's halls.

Larry Parker, KiMo general manager in 2018, said he's never seen a ghost in all his years at the KiMo. Rush Dudley, manager from 1984 to 2000, agrees. While some performers and technical crew members credit the paranormal for interventions and kindnesses, others blame the child-ghost.

According to Kathy Wagoner, "He is often blamed for production mistakes, bad luck, and typical paranormal activity – which seem to happen only when treats and toys are removed from a backstage "shrine" dedicated to the child."

Stewart Dawson has worked with lighting, set, and properties design for Opera Southwest and is the set designer, carpenter, and lighting engineer for New Mexico Young Actors. Stewart comments: "People claim that a stage light at the KiMo is left on for the boy ghost they say has been seen staring out the upstairs window. I've heard the overnight light called a ghost light, but for years many theatres have left a backstage light on for safety. The light was made famous by Emmett Kelly's "Weary Willie" skit, where he sweeps up the stage light. There are lots of practical reasons for having a light on in a dark theatre, including having light when staff comes in first thing in the morning. Has nothing to do with ghosts."

Filmmaker, film editor, and president of the New Mexico Post Alliance Brad Stoddart said, "Bobby? Everyone knows Bobby. You will hear stories from people more qualified than me. Although, we had an accident with a camera on a jib arm where I swear Bobby saved the day because we respected and gave him some trinkets."

Bobby: The Spirit of the KiMo

by Connie Spiegel

As a ballerina in the New Mexico Dance Company, I had performed on stages all over Albuquerque and up to Taos. Yet nothing prepared me for what I'd find when I first danced at the KiMo Theatre.

While the KiMo Theatre is a well-known icon in Albuquerque for its rich display of Southwestern art, you can hardly mention the KiMo Theatre without in the same breath, mentioning its ghostly history. This legendary theatre is said to be haunted by resident spirits; legends of the world beyond that roam its dimly lit hallways. The most famous and well-known of these Spirits is the young boy named Bobby.

I had heard all the weird talk about some ghost named Bobby, but I was too busy worrying about whether my bruised feet would hold up to think about ghosts. But once I was in the theatre and felt its strange magic, I began to wonder about this Bobby character.

The heavy wooden doors creaked as we entered the building. There is a slightly musty smell that hinted at the sodden history of this old lady of a venue. The entryway is dim with a slightly ominous ambiance. The quiet lighting, however, did not detract from the spooky-cool artwork that lines the aisles, right down to the red lights in the eyes of the cattle skulls. The intricate murals of small adobe pueblos and the Sandia Mountains spoke pure New Mexican. Bright, mosaic tiles in colorful, vibrant red and turquoise designs lined the walls and pillars, and making me feel as though we had traveled backward 100 years into native desert lands.

As we walked down the hall toward the dressing rooms, the natural light faded, and the atmosphere made every floor-creak ominous. Breathless, we continued to the performers' area, eagerly – and a bit nervously – seeking a view of what we had heard so much about. Finally, we came to the long white hallway that holds the dressing rooms, and we see it in its full spooky elegance: Bobby's shrine.

While the shrine is only a few feet high, it's an impressive sight. It's filled to the brim with gifts and offerings, ranging from ballet pointe shoes to candy bars, from letters and drawings to colorful toys. In the middle of it all is a small plate that holds two or three fresh glazed doughnuts.

A small sign was posted next to the collection that read: "Bobby's Shrine. This is an offering place for a resident spirit. Please treat it respectfully." The bountiful alter was put together over the years by performers in honor of Bobby Darnell, a young boy of six who killed in a tragic accident in the mid-1950s. Bobby–or rather, his spirit-is the renowned legend of the KiMo Theatre. All the performers know about Bobby and we were all aware of the trouble that can come from disrespecting the tiny-but-powerful ghost. And while the toys have been sitting on the shrine for years, fresh doughnuts are added by each new production.

On August 2, 1951, six-year-old Bobby Darnell accompanied friends, eleven year-old Lou Ellen and seven-year-old Ronald Ross to the KiMo to see *This Is America: They Fly with the Fleet*, a short documentary about US Naval Aviation. The theatre was crowded that day, with about 1000 in attendance to see the Abbott and Costello film *Comin' Round the Mountain*. However, tragedy struck when a boiler unexpectedly exploded in the lobby.

After the initial chaos, eight people were found to be injured. However, things took an even more tragic turn when the young Bobby was discovered to be dead. As it turns out, he had been spooked by something he had seen on the screen, and had run into the lobby just as the boiler exploded. The explosion had hurled him into a wall, crushing him. The events of this heartbreaking day were mourned respectfully throughout the city, and then peacefully left in the past. That is, until the return of Bobby in 1974.

* * *

It was just before Christmas in December of 1974, when New Mexico Repertory Theatre Company performed the theatre classic *A Christmas Carol*. Shortly before the show, director Andrew Shea noted some doughnuts mysteriously strung up against the wall behind the stage. Upon inquiring, he was informed that they were offerings for one Bobby Darnell, the young boy killed twenty years past. Shea, unaffected by the tall tale, ordered them removed and continued preparing for the show. However, it is then that things began to take a turn for the worst.

What happened that night was a compilation of unexplainable disasters; every theatre performer's nightmare. Performers tripped and stumbled or forgot their lines, lights failed or exploded, electrical cables and equipment fell down–and the list goes on. After the show, Shea promptly replaced the doughnuts, and miraculously, the following show went off without a hitch.

The doughnuts were left out, deemed as a necessary peace offering for the boisterous and lively Spirit of young Bobby.

The legend grew, even attracting local ghost hunters who, upon an investigation, depicted "wisps of energy" and even produced photos of a ghostly apparition.

Multiple sources claim to have seen a young boy, dressed in a striped t-shirt and blue jeans playing on the stairs of the lobby–directly above location of the boiler. Additionally, small bite marks were discovered in a number of the doughnuts strung along the ceiling. Later, more claims were made of sightings of a mysterious woman in a bonnet roaming the hallways at night; although little is known about her.

My experience performing on the famous KiMo stage was powerfully punctuated by the legend of Bobby and his tragic story. None of the dancers on our company actually saw Bobby, and thankfully, none of us were tripped. I thank the fresh glazed doughnuts for our safety.

However, my older autistic sister, Mari, claims she has twice seen Bobby running up and down the KiMo aisles. She insists she saw a small boy with light brown hair wearing a plaid shirt, blue jeans, and sneakers. Apparently Bobby changed his shirt.

These days the doughnuts are no longer strung along the walls backstage, as the shrine and the fresh doughnuts let him know the performers respect his right to roam the building. Bobby is considered a beloved friend of the performers. His story lives on as the legend of the KiMo Theatre.

New Mexico Young Actors

by Rick Nickerson

Founder, producer, director and instructor of New Mexico Young Actors from 1979-2014

When I first walked into the KiMo Theatre, I discovered that it was a unique, special place. With the Native American architecture and back lit skulls surrounding the top of the stage proscenium, I knew audiences would appreciate the unique beauty and significance of the theater.

Nickerson's Young Actors (NYA) was established in 1979 and, in May, 1980, performed the melodrama "Not Fit for Man or Beast" plus a mini-vaudeville show at the KiMo. My premier performers were thrilled when the school buses rolled up to the KiMo and 600 Albuquerque Public School children lined up to enter the theater. The vaudeville show and subsequent 1984 original production of "The Oldest Team in Vaudeville" shed light on the history of the KiMo Theatre. The KiMo had been a major venue for touring vaudeville acts during the 1930s and 1940s. After a two year renovation, NMY returned to the KiMo in 1984, where it established the theater as its permanent residence for major musical productions. NMY has continued to use the theater longer than any other local arts group.

In 1999, our theater company became a 501(C)3 non-profit organization and changed its name to New Mexico Young Actors (NMYA).

Thousands of young actors have participated with NMYA, a unique group that is designed for youth ages 9-19 playing all roles. NMYA performs four major productions a year; in the fall and spring a Broadway style musical is performed at the KiMo Theatre and also tours directly to schools performing children's theater classics. School tours are supported by city and state governments and The National Endowment for the Arts. This support enables NMYA to reach students who would otherwise be unable to attend productions. In its 39 years, NMYA has performed for over 500,000 youth!

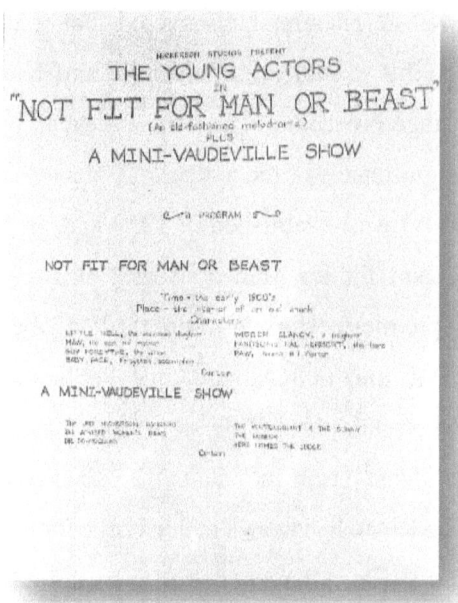

Playbill. *Not Fit for Man or Beast.* The Nickerson Young Actors. Circa 1980. Courtesy: Rick Nickerson. Photo credit: JMLoring.

NMYA has also provided opportunities for many young artists. In 1981, 17-year-old Robert Tate composed the music for two original productions, "Fat Sam's Grand Slam" and "Country Dreaming". 14-year-old David Dobrusky composed music for "Clowns" in 1983 and "The Oldest Team in Vaudeville" in 1984. NMYA has also taught several actors who have made theater their careers and actor Travis Ward-Osborne is currently performing on Broadway.

In partnership with the KiMo Theatre, NMYA continues to bring the delight and magic of theater to thousands of children every year!

Young Actor Composes at the KiMo Theatre

Seventeen-year-old Robert Tate composed music for *Fat Sam's Grand Slam* in 1981 and *Country Dreaming*, an original production, in 1982. For the 1982-1983 season, the NMYA performed *Clowns*. The book and lyrics were written by Rick Nickerson, with a musical score by fourteen- year-old David Dobrusky. Dobrusky also wrote the score for *The Oldest Team in Vaudeville* in 1984. At that time, Dobrusky attended Taylor Middle School in Albuquerque.

Dave did a superb job, he was in his fourth year with Nickerson Studios. He also appeared in the cast as Mr. Snobrich and Senator Schmuck.

I was honored to have met and worked with these amazing young artists.

Playbill. *Pippi Longstocking*. Albuquerque Young Actors. Circa 2009. Courtesy: Rick Nickerson.
Credit: JMLoring.

New Mexico Young Actors
by Paul Bower

For twenty years, Paul Bower has worked as a freelance singer, director, conductor, and teacher in Albuquerque. He joined New Mexico Young Actors as principal music director in 2004. A professional opera singer, Bower was appointed executive director of NMYA in January 2015. Bower runs the business side of the company as well as directing, casting, and producing most of the shows. NMYA has been providing theatre arts training through drama classes and productions of plays and musicals for children by children in the Albuquerque region since 1979.

New Mexico Young Actors (NMYA) has touched tens of thousands of children with the power of drama, music, and dance. Our students find a creative outlet for their talents and a means of expressing themselves in a supportive and welcoming environment. Our audiences, ranging from toddlers to seniors, frequently express a mild surprise that such a quality product can come from mere children.

We have performed our musicals at the KiMo Theatre since 1980. The theatre offers just the right space for our productions and our students always enjoy the historical and architectural aspects of the building. In addition to our weekend public performances, we offer weekday field trip performances for schoolchildren, teachers, and parent chaperones. We will often reach the KiMo seating capacity, giving us a thrilling sold-out performance!

Between 14,000 and 16,000 people attend our performances each year. In addition to our musical productions at the KiMo, we offer drama classes and play productions, which we take on tour to local schools.

New Mexico Young Actors receives strong support from the Albuquerque community through grants and contributions. Our company also offers good-paying contract work to many area professionals, including designers, musicians, and engineers. Our cadre of volunteers fills roles such as ushers, stage crew, props managers, child wranglers, drivers, and other important positions and can number into the hundreds each season. Most of our volunteers are parents of children in the program and some of our volunteers and staff are former students in NMYA.

Stephanie Bauer was onstage in productions at the KiMo before working as our stage manager for nearly two decades. Lee Megill played roles in more than a dozen shows before becoming secretary and assistant director with the company. Kaylee Hammond is an actress who performed in our musicals and is now a member of our Board of Directors. Joshua Megill was a little boy in our productions for a decade who is now our company choreographer.

Our students love performing at the KiMo. They find it fascinating, invigorating, and fun--especially the very young ones. Most of them have never been in a big stage production. The excitement and energy are palpable when we begin rehearsing and then performing on the big stage.

NMYA Pit Band

NMYA uses a small instrumental ensemble, or pit band, of three or four players for its KiMo performances. One of our goals is for our musicals to always be performed with a live band. It is a rich experience for our actors to work with live music and it offers flexibility with the score.

New Mexico Young Actors Become Adult Professionals

Several NMYA students have established careers in the arts. Many can be found in conservatories and university music and theater departments across the country and some students are working on Broadway and in film. While some make their homes in New York or Los Angeles, many have found a wonderful niche in the thriving community theater scene of Albuquerque.

David Dobrusky was a student from 1982 to 1984. In 2017, he was nominated as "Best Musical Director" for production in San Francisco. Alumna Sarin West graduated from Oklahoma City University with a degree in Theatre Arts and is currently in NYU's graduate acting class of 2020. Sarin was in productions of *Cinderells'a Glass Slipper*, *Honk, Jr.*, and *Pippi Longstocking* in 2008—2009.

Travis Ward-Osborne, who performed in *Pippi Longstocking* in 2003, and in *The Magic Mrs. Piggle Wiggle* in 2004, is currently performing in *Aladdin* on Broadway. Stafford Douglas, who performed in *Cinderella's Glass Slipper* in 2008, has appeared in several local films.

Joliana Davidson, who played Cinderella in *Cinderella's Glass Slipper* in 2015, was chosen as the recipient of the Popejoy Award in 2016. The prize is awarded to one male and one female Albuquerque area high school theater performer and includes an all-expenses paid trip to New York City for a week of training with theater professionals culminating in a national competition. Joliana was a high school freshman and the youngest to ever win the award.

A list of productions from 1979 to 2017 appears on the New Mexico Young Actors website. In addition to original productions like *Clowns* (1983) and *Country Dreaming* (1982, 1986, 1991), recent productions include: *Alice in Wonderland, Jr.*, 2016; *Annie, Jr.*, 2012; *Beauty and the Beast, Jr.*, 2011; *Big Bad*, 2015; *Doc, Doc, Goose!*, 2015; *The Frog Princess*, 2013; *Jack and the Giant*, 2015; *James and the Giant Peach, Jr.*, 2017; *The Pied Piper of Hamelin*, 2012; *Pocahontas*, 2016; *Puss in Boots*, 2013; *Silver's Secret*, 2017; *Snow Queen*, 2016; *Snow White & Seven Dwarfs*, 2014; *The Three Bully Goats Griff*, 2016.

New Mexico Young Actors: http://www.nmyoungactors.org/#Home

Auditorium. Audience at *Pippi Longstocking*. Albuquerque Young Actors.
Circa 2003. Photo credit: Rick Nickerson.

Joliana Davidson won the Popejoy Award in 2016. She played Cinderella in *Cinderella's Glass Slipper* at the KiMo in April 2015. For the Popejoy award, judges go to state high schools and attend performances and nominate a student. One girl and one boy travel to New York City, all expenses paid, where they are trained by NYC professionals and compete for the Jimmy Awards. Joliana was a freshman, the youngest to ever win and travel to New York.

New Mexico Young Actors' list of productions at the KiMo is impressive. Their website boasts, "Proudly sponsored by New Mexico Arts, a division of the Department of Cultural Affairs and the National Endowment of the Arts."

A list of productions from 1979 to 2017 appears on the New Mexico Young Actors website. Besides older productions like *Clowns* (1983) and *Country Dreaming* (1982, 1986, 1991) our website lists dozens of newer productions, including: *Alice in Wonderland, Jr.*, 2016; *Annie, Jr.* 2007, 2012; *Beauty and the Beast, Jr.*, 2011; *Big Bad*, 2015; *Doc, Doc, Goose!*, 2015; *The Frog Princess*, 2002, 2003, 2008, 2013; *Jack and the Giant*, 2000, 2006, 2015; *James and the Giant Peach, Jr.*, 2017; *The Pied Piper of Hamelin*, 2012; *Pocahontas*, 2016; *Puss in Boots*, 2013; *Silver's Secret* 2017, *Snow Queen* 2016, *Snow White & Seven Dwarfs* (Musical) 1998, 2003, 2014; *The Three Bully Goats Griff*, 2016.

New Mexico Young Actors: http://www.nmyoungactors.org/#Home

Growing Up at the KiMo

By David Zamora

David Zamora was the son of PAZ, the Ehecatl Aztec Dancers' leader and historian.

My first memories of dancing at the KiMo Theatre? I was pretty young. I remember the Folklorico dancers in one dressing room and the Aztec dancers in another.

My mother, Rita Zamora, and my father, PAZ, always danced with Baile at various functions throughout the decades and my sisters, Rosa, Luna, Crystal, and I joined them. I remember waiting to dance, then climbing the stairs, seeing the *nicho* with all the stuff people had left through the years, wondering what each piece represented.

My most recent memory was performing for Amy Biehl High School's graduation (we've performed for every graduation ceremony they have had. My sister was part of their first graduating class). This time I climbed the stairs still wondering about the story behind each piece in the famous *nicho*. This time, however, I was carrying my daughter up the stairs in her car seat so she could be just offstage where my wife, Kathleen Garcia, could watch her as she drummed. I was a proud papa knowing my daughter, Flor Zamora, would be a new generation to dance at the historic KiMo Theatre.

Ballet Repertory Theatre of New Mexico. Rehearsal. Circa 2017.
Courtesy: Ballet Repertory Theatre of New Mexico.
Photo credit: Katherine Giese.

The Ballet Repertory Theatre of New Mexico Preamble

For almost thirty years, the Ballet Repertory Theatre of New Mexico has been known as "the ballet company at the KiMo Theatre." According to their web site, "Ballet Theatre of New Mexico began in the fall of 1989 with the creation of its junior company. By the fall of 1991, Ballet Theatre produced its first senior company production, A Victorian Christmas. In 1996, Ballet Theatre announced its first full season, which included the full-length production of The Nutcracker. Since that time, the repertory has grown to include a richly varied selection of pieces—from great 18th--19th century classical ballets to contemporary masterpieces of today—that demonstrate the expertise and versatility of each individual dancer. To better reflect this wide array of choreography, in the summer of 2007 Ballet Theatre changed its name to Ballet Repertory Theatre.

Ballet Repertory Theatre of New Mexico

by Katherine Giese

Katherine Giese, has been with the Ballet Repertory Theatre for over twenty-one years. She is the company's executive director and artistic director. Before 2004, she was a professional dancer, teacher, choreographer, and volunteer with the company.

Over the years, Ballet Repertory Theatre has worked hard to become the premier ballet company for Albuquerque. Just like Albuquerque, we are truly being unique. Every year, the company expands its repertoire and reaches new audiences, joyously demonstrating its mastery of both classics and innovative works. For a grant, I researched our ticket sales, and in one season audiences were coming from twenty of the thirty-three New Mexico counties to attend our performances at the KiMo Theatre. We share our passion for ballet at the historic KiMo Theatre. Nationally, if a ballet company produces *Swan Lake,* it is a very popular attraction due to it being such an acclaimed ballet, but locally our audiences are families with younger children, and what sells is story ballets with themes children are already familiar with. When we produced *Swan Lake* it was popular, but it did not come close to the sold-out audiences we have had for our story ballets that have familiar stories, like *Alice in Wonderland* and *Beauty & the Beast*. I love exposing and educating our audiences to the classics, but introducing kids to the live art of ballet and the KiMo Theatre is the best part of running BRT.

Ballet Repertory Theatre of New Mexico. Circa 2017.
Courtesy: Ballet Repertory Theatre of New Mexico.
Photo credit: Katherine Giese.

Ballet Repertory Theatre of New Mexico. Family looks into the pit while orchestra sets up. Circa 2017. Courtesy: Ballet Repertory Theatre of New Mexico. Photo credit: Rush Dudley.

The first year our students dance at the KiMo, they are pretty excited. Kids can audition starting at the age of nine. Their first year to be in *The Nutcracker* or one of the other story ballets is so magical for them.

On the first night of rehearsals in the theatre we do a tour of the KiMo with them so they know the rules of the theatre. The older dancers who have been through this for a couple of years are so eager to do the tours themselves. 'Can we take them? Can we? Come on, let us do the tour!'

They take them downstairs, maybe fifty kids. 'This is Bobby's shrine.' They tell the kids who he is and what they have to do. And then, 'This is stage right. This is the men's dressing room. This is the pit.' The older kids tell the first-timers where the doors are. That's mostly about safety. They tell them how to get around backstage. The older kids love to do it and the younger kids are in awe. Yes, the first day every year at the KiMo it's always cool to see the kids looking around backstage and looking out into the seats where the audience and their families will be.

Last year, we had this little boy who hadn't been in the KiMo before. He kept saying, 'Oh, my gosh. This is amazing. This is amazing. I had no idea. It's like flat!' He was taken with the theatre and the backdrops, and he was surprised the backdrop was a flat piece of canvas painted to look like 3-D scenery.

My favorite part about dancing at the KiMo, and it's the same for a lot of the dancers, comes after the children's series shows. Ballet Repertory Theatre's Children's Series is part of our Education Outreach Program, where we present hour-long performances designed to introduce children to the magic of theatre and dance. Because we believe in the value of our outreach program, we ask school administrators and teachers to excuse our younger dancers from school to perform in these daytime performances. The schools have been great and supportive of allowing students to perform. Performances are attended mostly by elementary-school-age children, and after each performance, as the audience is excused from their seats school by school, the kids get to meet all the ballet characters out in the front of the KiMo. That part's so cool, the way all the children's eyes are so wide and full of wonder and awe

We even have a bus that drives in from Grants, New Mexico.

We like the setting of the KiMo, it's an intimate, cozy, atmosphere where audiences can feel the connection to the performers and the story on stage.

Ballet Repertory Theatre of New Mexico: www.brtnm.com

Ballet Repertory Theatre of New Mexico. Circa 2017.
Courtesy: Ballet Repertory Theatre of New Mexico.
Photo credit: Katherine Giese.

Letter to the Ballet Repertory Theatre of New Mexico

March 6, 2017

Dear Friends,

On Tuesday, February 28th, I had the opportunity to accompany a group of children from Lew Wallace Elementary School to the KiMo Theatre. We went to see your production of "Coppelia" and came away thoroughly enchanted!

Over the years, I have had the pleasure of attending many productions at the KiMo but "Coppelia" was by far the most engaging I have experienced! I enjoyed listening to the students discuss the ballet and the fifth-grade boys were exclaiming over the leaps of the dancers while the little girls loved the beautiful costumes. I was especially pleased to see that although the children did not know the story of "Coppelia," they understood the story through the music, sets and the characters on stage. That is true storytelling!

Thank you for giving us the tickets and the opportunity to attend the ballet at the KiMo. The theatre itself is one of Albuquerque's jewels but the experience our students had in seeing a top-notch production was a gift that we will not soon forget.

Sincerely,

Cheryl Inskeep

Cheryl Inskeep Librarian
Lew Wallace Elementary School

Managing the KiMo Theatre

by Rush Dudley

Rush Dudley was the manager of the KiMo Theatre from 1985 to 2000. He graduated from the University of New Mexico Theatre Department, after studying stage lighting and set design as well as front-of-house operations. Over the next eight years, he designed for the Santa Fe Opera, the New Orleans Opera, and Rollins College of Winter Park, Fla., among other producing theatres.

The KiMo manager is part of a team. My job was to create an environment so the audience could have the experience of seeing artists work in a building owned by the city government with high standards of safety. I worked face to face with artists, and sometimes they had strong convictions about their work and how it had to be presented, but as the manager, I had to make sure that what they wanted fit into the city's guidelines for the building. People sometimes did not understand the stage is an industrial work area governed by fire and building codes, and by OSHA (Occupational Safety and Health Administration), an agency of the U.S. Department of Labor).

In a theatre, you have actors, heavy equipment, construction, lots of electricity, and movement. And an audience. There's a lot going on. The building was a rental. You would get the use of the building, the use of the technical equipment, and one stage person whose main job was to create a safe environment for performers and audience.

When I worked at the KiMo, the city had one well-trained person with years of lighting, sound, and set design experience in the building who knew how to run the theatre as a safe and orderly operation. But I didn't work twenty-four hours a day. A group like the Opera could set up and rehearse twelve hours a day for several days before a performance, and a city employee was required to be in the building.

In the 1970s, there were grants available to train theatre people. Sally Opel got a grant and provided a place for young people to get technical training, singers, musicians, stage hands. Sally also got an apprentice program grant.

My job was to support performers in a professional and responsible way. I worked with Rick Nickerson's young actors and with the Opera folks. I volunteered some of my time to do lighting. When I became theatre manager, I had to stop helping. They often had to bring in their own people. After I left the KiMo, I designed some sets for Ramon Flores, who was producing La Compañía shows, and other performing groups, but I was off the city's clock.

Funny things happen when you are the manager of a large theatre. Once a New Zealand group went out and collected dead wood and wanted to build a live fire mid-stage during their performance. During rehearsal, without asking anybody, they lit the fire and all the smoke detectors went off. I had to explain to the artist that the City of Albuquerque owned the building and there were fire and building codes that they had to work with.

Outreach into the Community

In the 1990s, Albuquerque had its crime problems just like other growing American cities. Between 1993 and 1997, Mayor Martin Chavez made it his mission to make changes in Albuquerque. The Youth Development Incorporated (YDI) people got funding to offer arrested and troubled kids alternatives. If a kid got arrested, he could go to YDI and learn life skills. It is an excellent program. Every year, YDI produced a play. They'd hire a playwright to write a play about subjects kids understood. They would perform them at the KiMo.

One year, YDI partnered with a group called Working Classrooms to write and stage a play. This particular play was about restoring the family. We had 700 gang kids, fifteen police, social workers, and city employees at the play. The playwright was a genius who wove comedy into the story.

Part of my job as KiMo manager was to be in the lobby during a performance. That day I was in the back of the audience and all I could hear was these kids laughing. They left their lives outside. Seven hundred kids watching and laughing. Together. That's the power of theatre. It's a living thing. Seven hundred kids that day became children again and they were all deeply involved in the story.

A Celebration of Unity in 1992

by Jacqueline Murray Loring

The September 24, 1992 "A Celebration of Unity 1692 to 1992" invitation to supporters is signed by Verna Williamson-Teller, Isleta Pueblo, Co-Chair and Jaime Chávez, Atrisco Pueblo, Co-Chair.

In part the invitation reads, "...When we look to the past we learn more about who we are now and what our place in the world means. The Pueblo of Isleta celebrated the Year of Indigenous Peoples in honor and memory of our loved ones who struggle to preserve the sacredness of our culture..."

Among the archived booklets and flyers announcing events at the KiMo Theatre belonging to historian Rudy Miera are two announcing "A Celebration of Unity". One event listed for September 24, 1992 took place at the Isleta Pueblo Lakes. The other was held two weeks later on October 7, 1992 at the KiMo Theatre.

According to Isleta Tribal elder and environmental activist Verna Williamson-Teller, these celebrations occurred as the Isleta Pueblo received approval from the Environmental Protection Agency (EPA) of their water quality standards for the Rio Grande River. The project required all upstream users to abide by the Tribe's high water quality standards.

"During our (Isleta Pueblo) work," Williamson-Teller said, "we connected with the Atrisco people on our common goal to have a healthy river. We worked together educating people on what it meant to have river water quality and why the Isleta people were working so hard to develop standards. The Atrisco people were helpful. They did some of the ground work because they were doing a lot work on environmental issues and on the Atrisco Land Grant of 1692."

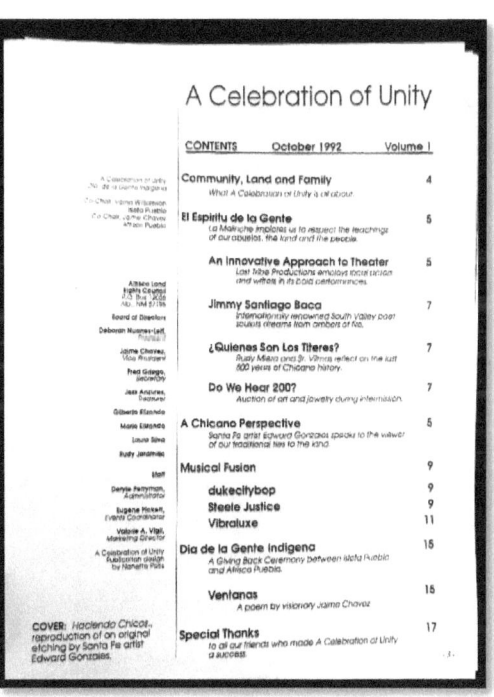

Celebration of Unity 1692 to 1992 booklet

Booklet. Celebration of Unity. Contents page. Circa 1992.
Courtesy: Rudy Miera. Photo credit: Rudy Miera

Booklet page. A Celebration of Unity. Circa 1992.
Courtesy: Rudy Miera. Photo credit: Rudy Miera.

When asked about the event's booklet title, "Isleta Pueblo-Atrisco Pueblo," Williamson-Teller said, "It could be argued that there isn't technically an Atrisco Pueblo, not one of the Nineteen Pueblos, but here we recognized the historic, indigenous, ancestral connection to the peoples who came from Mexico. The Spanish word for village is pueblo. The use of the term "Atrisco Pueblo" for the unity celebrations was mostly ceremonial, historical.

On September 24, 1992 at the Isleta Pueblo Lakes, we brought our harvests together at a "Giving Back Ceremony", Williamson-Teller said. "Two weeks later, we invited the whole community to join us in the celebration." The event was sponsored by the Atrisco Land Rights Council.

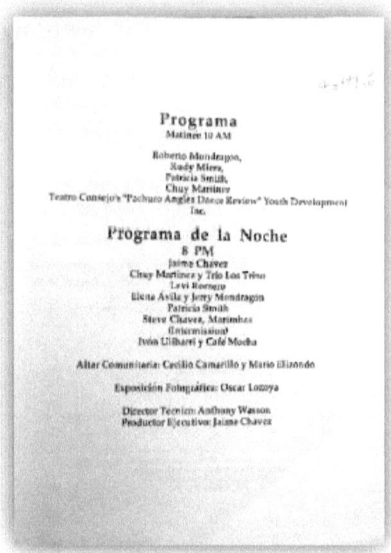

Booklet.
Celebration of
Unity page.

Programa. Circa 1992.

Courtesy: Rudy Miera. Photo credit: Rudy Miera.

According to the booklet for the October 7th celebration, "The Giving Back Ceremony symbolically returns to Isleta Pueblo from the Atrisco community the sustenance its ancestors provided to the settlers in the Rio Grande by honoring a feast in honor of the Pueblo." Included on October 7th was a lecture at the KiMo Theatre on the survival of Indigenous people of the Americas and an art and jewelry show. Lost Tribes Productions showed scenes from several of their plays. Internationally known poet Jimmy Santiago Baca read his poems. Rudy Miera held a puppet presentation with a puppet character, *El Viejo Vilmas*, a symbol of the respected village elders of the Hispanic community. The programs at the KiMo were open to the public in the evenings with special daytime performances designed for field trips for public school students.

Another program booklet for the KiMo Theatre celebration reads: The program at the KiMo Theatre included the "Dia de la Gente Indigena-A Giving Back Ceremony" between Isleta Pueblo and Atrisco Pueblo and included Musical Fusion featuring Dukecitybop, Steele Justice, and Vibraluxe. Santa Fe Artist Edward Gonzales presented "A Chicano Perspective" that "speaks to the viewer of our traditional ties to the land."

A CELEBRATION OF UNITY
KIMO THEATRE-WEDNESDAY, OCT. 7, 1992 8:00 pm

EL ESPIRITU DE LA GENTE -- 500 YEARS
THE SPIRIT OF THE PEOPLE.....

A HARD LOOK AT NEW MEXICO'S PAST;
A VISION OF HOPE FOR THE FUTURE

FEATURING: MUSIC, THEATRE & POETRY
 * JIMMY SANTIAGO BACA, POET
 * JAIME CHAVEZ, POET
 * RUDY MIERA, PUPPETEER
 * LOST TRIBE PRODUCTIONS

SPONSOR: ATRISCO LAND RIGHTS COUNCIL
TICKETS: $5.00 AT TICKETMASTER OUTLETS OR AT THE DOOR

Celebration of Unity flyer. Circa 1992. Courtesy: Rudy Miera.
Photo Credit: Rudy Miera

KiMo Theatre: Fact and Folklore

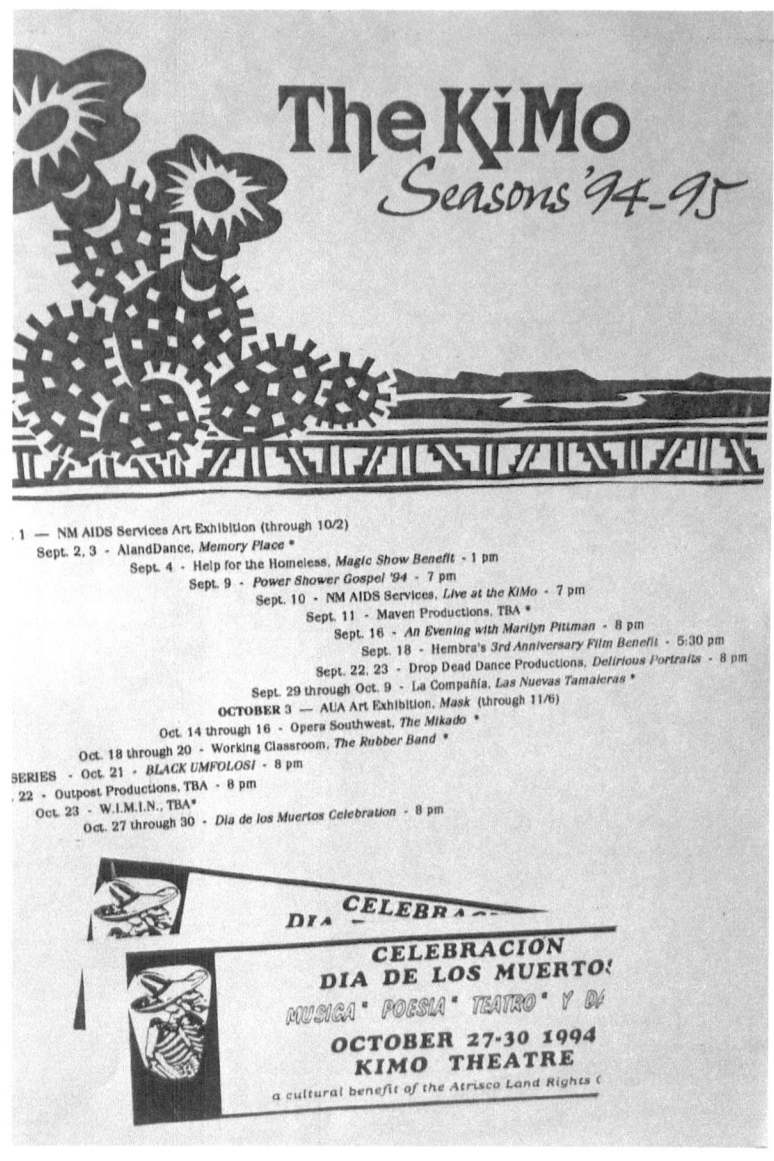

Flyer. Kimo Seasons 1994 and 1995. Courtesy: Rudy Miera.
Photo Credit: Rudy Miera. 1994--1995 Day of the Dead Celebrations

El Día de Los Muertos (The Day of the Dead) is celebrated on November 1st and 2nd to remember those who have departed. Families and friends honor the dead in joyful celebrations, build altars, prepare special foods, and hold parades where children carry yellow marigolds.

Actor/Teacher Rudy Miera said, "Previously, before the 1990s, people didn't do many public displays. They would go with family to the graves of relatives and bring food and drink, maybe offerings and sing, pray, and converse. The idea of open, public celebrations came about at the KiMo. In recent years, these celebrations have combined into the Marigold Festival Parade in Albuquerque's South Valley."

Booklet. Day of the Dead celebration. Celebración Dia De Los Muertos. Circa 1996. Courtesy: Rudy Miera. Photo credit: JMLoring.

Flyer. Celebración Dia De Los Muertos. Circa 1996.
Courtesy: Rudy Miera. Photo by Rudy Miera. 1994

The KiMo Theatre played host to the Celebración--Día de Los Muertos, October 27 to 30, 1994. According to Miera, students on the Thursday and Sunday matinee programs were treated to poetry readings from Cecilio Garcia-Camarillo, Jaime Chávez, Doris Fields, and Rudolfo Anaya. Music ranged from marimba instrumentals by Steve Chávez, traditional folk music by Bayou Seco, Native American rock music by the group Paintings to original and traditional *corridos* and *canciones* by popular *guitarista* and singer Jesús "Chuy" Martinez. There were also theatrical scenes presented by Jerry Mondragón and the late, respected *curandera* Elena Ávila.

The Friday and Saturday programs included encore performances of the two-act play *Día de Los Muertos*, written by Miera and directed by Nita Luna. The play had previously been staged in the Experimental Theatre at the University of New Mexico. The four-day cultural feast at the KiMo was a benefit for the Atrisco Land Rights Council.

The dedication on the program flyer reads: "El Dia de Los Muertos is dedicated to all of our ancestors who have gone before us. It is here produced with special thanks to San José Parish." (Flyer provided courtesy of Rudy J. Miera.)

Miera recalled another event. "On November 1, 1996, the public Día de Los Muertos commemoration included a morning program for students that featured (former Lieutenant Governor and bilingual advocate) Roberto Mondragón singing songs, poetry readings by Patricia Smith (from Detroit), and music by Jesús "Chuy" Martinez. A special modern dance program was presented by Teatro Consejo's Pachuco Angels Dance Review from Youth Development Inc.

For the evening program, audiences were treated to poetry by Levi

Romero (from Dixon, N.M.), Jaime Chávez from Carnuel, N.M., and music by Chuy Martinez now joined by Los Trinos. Elena Ávila and Jerry Mondragón performed theatrical scenes, Steve Chávez played the marimba, and Ivón Ulibarri y Café Mocha closed out the program with their style of dynamic salsa music.

Miera said, "Of special historical significance is the fact that an *altar comunitaria* (community altar) was organized and set up in the lobby by Cecilio Garcia-Camarillo and Mario Elizondo. This altar, incorporating photographs of departed loved ones, treats once enjoyed by the deceased (tamales, tortillas, and more), and sugar skulls, etc., was on display for viewing. Contributions by visitors were also welcomed. The importance of this altar is that it was likely the first-ever public display of a Day of the Dead *ofrenda* (offering) in New Mexico, as this is an old Mexican tradition that has been more recently adopted by Chicanos in New Mexico, and it took place in the lobby of the KiMo Theatre. Of special cultural significance is that PAZ and his Mexica/Aztec dance group, Ehecatl, moved their outdoor ceremonial dances to the indoor stage of the KiMo Theatre, starting each performance with their Blessing to the Four Directions while burning copal, the traditional incense; employing dance, drums, and ancient prayers that echoed in the old Pueblo Deco performance palace."

According to PAZ, leader of the Mexica/Aztec dance group Ehecatl, "In 1994, Jaime Chávez asked us to dance at the KiMo's Day of the Dead celebration. We also danced at the graduations of Amy Biehl Charter High School in Albuquerque."

Miera concluded, "From the Michael Jackson-style group dances of the Pachuco Angels Dance Review to the depiction of visiting spirits on the Day of the Dead, from the poetry of land and water protection by Jaime Chávez to the dynamics of Hispanic male/female relationships as presented by Elena Ávila and Jerry Mondragón, political issues, family humor, and the psychological scars left by colonialism have all found expression in live performance on the KiMo stage. From commemorating many of life's struggles and achievements to celebrating the lives of our ancestors who have gone on to a new life, a magnificent variety of New Mexican performers have had a welcome home to act, dance, and sing about the memorable events on the stage at the KiMo Theatre."

Links:

Ehecatl Aztec Dancers: http://www.ehecatlaztecdancers.com/index.html
Opera Southwest: http://www.operasouthwest.org/operas
Working Classrooms:
http://www.workingclassroom.org/about-us/historyus/history

Flyer. El Sueño de Navidad del Santero. Circa 1970s. Courtesy: Rudy Miera. Photo credit: JMLoring.

An Albuquerque Poet Remembers

by Don McIver

Don McIver is a poet, writer, rhetor, monologist, dudeist priest. donmciver.blogspot.com @theDonofABQ.

I've been involved in a number of events at the KiMo Theatre over the years. It's a pretty special place. I hope someone has mentioned the altar in the basement, as I generally gather myself there before the shows begin.

I hosted and facilitated a reading in support of Bill Nevins on September 14, 2003. He'd been fired from Rio Rancho Public Schools because one of his students read an anti-war poem over the public address system (PA). There were about thirty poets who read in support of him. Some of the participants at Nevins's reading were Jenny Bird; Chuy Martinez; Demetria Martinez; Manuel Gonzales (2016-18 Albuquerque poet laureate); and Danny Solis.

Patricia Smith, nationally known spoken-word performer, playwright, and author did a reading at the KiMo as fundraiser for the National Poetry Slam (NPS) in 2005.

I also hosted numerous poetry finals at the KiMo Theatre for the Southwest Shootout (SWSO). The SWSO is a regional poetry slam that brings together teams from the Southwest to compete every summer and prepare for the National Poetry Slam. Albuquerque has hosted the Southwest Shootout (in fact started it in 2002), and over the years we've used the KiMo for finals on numerous occasions, most recently on June 15, 2013.

As for SWSO, we had teams from Denver, Austin, Dallas, Houston, Phoenix, Flagstaff, Colorado Springs, and many more. Hakim Bellamy, who later became Albuquerque's inaugural poet laureate (2012-14), was on a few teams that read as part of SWSO, as was Jessica Lopez, 2014-16 Albuquerque poet laureate.

Slam champion Janae Johnson won her Women of the World Poetry Slam title at the KiMo in 2015. And on February 10, 2017, I participated in a staged reading of Joseph Moncure March's 'The Wild Party' as a fundraiser for the New Mexico Film Foundation. The reading was staged with a live band, some burlesque dancers, and a 1920s theme. The poem itself is very long, with about eight readers each reading a couple of pages. Like I say, the KiMo is a really special place, especially for poetry."

KiMo Theatre. At twilight. Circa 2000s. Courtesy: KiMo Theatre.

Introduction to the Twilight in the KiMo Theatre

The KiMo Theatre hosted "An Evening for Vietnam" as a fundraiser for TwoBricks's music school in Vietnam on Saturday, October 10, 2015. TwoBricks is an Albuquerque-based not-for-profit whose mission is to build schools in underdeveloped regions. The evening featured the showing of **Same Same but Different**, *a documentary about "the goodness of humans, the grace of forgiveness, and the power of redemption," according to the event website. It was created by New Mexico filmmakers Deryle Perryman and Moisés González. A concert by singer/songwriter Terry Allen and his son, Bukka Allen, followed the film.*

For most of the audience the experience of watching **Same Same but Different** *is made finer by a heart-pounding and sometimes heart-wrenching soundtrack by musicians Terry Allen, Harry Manx, Greyhound Soul, Roxy Gordon, and Vietnam veteran Jim Hagerman. For writer, poet, editor, and SouthWest Writers member Pamela Yenser, it was life-affecting. Here is her story.*

Twilight in the KiMo Theatre

by Pamela Yenser

What began as movie, a beer, and a good cause became a strange all-night event I will never forget. My husband and I often take Route 66 downtown for sushi and a movie, but that night Kelly and I had a hamburger at a café near the KiMo, Albuquerque's Pueblo Deco picture palace. We had purchased tickets front and center for a fundraising event. Our friend Deryle Perryman, a Vietnam veteran and filmmaker, was showing a Kickstarter film he and Albuquerque cinematographer Moisés González had recently produced.

Their film, *Same Same But Different*, is based on interviews with veterans who have gone back to Vietnam to make moral—and physical—reparations. One current Perryman project is a building for a music school. This personal documentary, punctuated by bursts of war footage, was part of a program said to feature Santa Fe singer/songwriter Terry Allen*. I saw the film, but never heard the music.

KiMo Theatre: Fact and Folklore

As the film credits rolled, the war-drum lights on the ceiling came up, and—above heavy velvet curtains—the amber eyes of many buffalo skulls mounted across the stage proscenium turned red, symbolic of life's final setting sun. As I bent to retrieve my beer cup and my purse, I realized that some of that flashing was coming from inside my head.

(I sympathize with surviving veterans and those affected families here and abroad who suffer daily from the ravages of war—chemical burns, internal injuries, loss of eyes, limbs, and worse, and traumatic brain injury [TBI]. I'm familiar with the symptoms of TBI—disorienting triggers of noise and light, sleep deprivation, hallucinations, dyslexic spelling, and word-finding. On the way to work one day, I was rear-ended. A coup-contre coup injury resulted. For the rest of the schoolyear, I could not find my classes or the ends of my sentences. I've been left less aware, but more perceptive; hopeful, and yet permanently impaired. I speak in spoonerisms, apologizing to students for my writing: "It looks like kitchens crashing." I mean, "Chicken scratching!" I've retired. Now a writer-editor, I depend on a thesaurus to reconnoiter the semantic trails of my broken brain.)

I was dizzy from standing too quickly at intermission, but trudged up the stairs toward the foyer. I spotted a friend, nurse Jacqueline Loring, in the last row, and collapsed next to her for help. Kelly joined us in the remaining aisle seat and began to talk with her. I interrupted.

"I can't see and I need water, now." Kelly thought I would be okay but Jacqueline, married to a Vietnam vet and known for smart screenwriting and good causes, called for an ambulance.

The next thing I knew, an EMT was pointing a flashlight in my face. "Look into my eyes," he said.

"But I can't see you," I whispered. "Everything is gray with leopard spots."

In the twilight of intermission at the KiMo Theatre, I was surrounded by soldiers in camouflage rolling me onto a gurney before night fell. I woke up in an ambulance with tubes and wires running from my body. During my intake at the hospital, I was awakened and asked to identify myself and where I was when I experienced my blackout.

"I was in the KiMo Theatre." "Oh, we're so sorry to hear that."

"That's okay. I'm feeling better now."

"In the operating theatre? Where were you cut?"

"Pardon?" I pictured surgical knives. "I fainted at the KiMo Theatre—downtown." "Oh, we thought 'chemo operating theatre,' so we're moving you to a room."

I said, "That's great. There's usually a long wait."

Evidently that "chemo theatre" entry at intake caused confusion among the nurses, who woke me throughout the night, looking at my chart, opening my gown, and lowering my covers, looking for the war on cancer that, for me, never happened.

For more information about the event, see http://ampconcerts.org/event/222201/an-evening-for- vietnam and http://www.kimotickets.com/event/222146.

*For more information about Terry Allen, see http://terryallenartmusic.com

The Grande Dame

by Author Anne Hillerman

Anne Hillerman is a journalist, reporter, author and the daughter of western writer Tony Hillerman. In 2013, Anne's debut novel, Spider Woman's Daughter, continued to develop the beloved characters from her father's Joe Leaphorn mystery series. Anne's fourth book in the series, Cave of Bones, was released in April 2018.

The KiMo, the Grande Dame of New Mexico theatres, wears her age splendidly. I never imagined that I would stand on that graceful stage, but life has a way of handing us surprises.

When I made the switch from journalism to writing books, I soon realized that the transition also involved speaking before an audience. As an author, my audience usually consists of a few people in folding chairs in the community room of a library, or a cluster of potential fans at Bookworks, Page One or Treasure House books.

Then, the Friends of the Albuquerque Bernalillo County Library System suggested a fund-raising idea in conjunction with the release of my first novel.

I agreed not only because of the good work they do to keep our libraries going, but because the plan involved using the KiMo as a venue. The wheels started turning and next thing I knew, it was show time.

Up to that point, I'm embarrassed to say, I had never even set foot in the theatre, but its reputation shone brightly all the way up here to where I live in Santa Fe. To combat my stage fright, I had enlisted the help of drama students from the New Mexico School for the Arts to do selected readings from my mystery. I was happy to have the company of these perky teenagers and, because they really want to be performers, they loved the idea.

That evening, our one-night-only performance had a wonderful energy to it. The amazing Pueblo Deco Dream design style of the interior, the wrought iron birds and the glowing eyes of the buffalo charmed me. Unlike my experience with some other appearances, the microphones worked, the lights came on as they should, and there were no issues with the heat or the air conditioning. The staff smiled as they helped us.

Standing on stage in that beautiful, unique theatre was so joyous, I forgot to be nervous. Thank you, KiMo, for adding an overlay of fun to a special night.

The Alvarado Follies at the KiMo

by Mary E. Dorsey

Dorsey is a writer, poet and SouthWest Writer's member.

Nestled on a quiet, tree-filled patch of Albuquerque's North Valley is the older and much beloved Alvarado Elementary School. This school had the reputation of having a close-knit community where staff and parents worked closely together for the betterment of all its students. As with most public schools, it too needed fundraisers to assure that each student received the supplies and occasional field trips that made education interesting and fun.

The biggest and most famous of these fundraisers was known as the Alvarado Follies—a yearly fun-filled variety show written and performed by the staff and parents. This show meant hard work and many hours of rehearsals to ensure a quality show for all who attended. What elevated this show was the fact that it was done in a real theatre—the famous KiMo Theatre. For many years, one weekend in March, the KiMo became the setting for this fun activity. Parents, friends, family, students, and dignitaries dressed up and attended this show as though it were a Broadway production.

In the late 1980s, I was the school's nurse and therefore had the opportunity to become a part of this festive occasion. All those involved worked hard to present a quality and fun variety show. Writing scripts for skits, practicing dance numbers, and helping when necessary took many weeks but was worth it in the end. The KiMo had the feel and look of a grand theatre and gave the whole project the professional touch that elevated it from 'not bad' to 'absolutely fab!'

The green room downstairs would bustle with activity. The many well-lighted mirrors made for easy preparation before going onstage. Butterflies would flit in nervous stomachs while waiting for the iconic velvet curtains to open, only to disappear as soon as the performance began.

Hearing the applause of the appreciative audience made us feel like real Broadway stars. The KiMo had a magic all its own. It gave a sense of elegance to the many productions it has seen over the years. Although I am now retired from the school system, I shall never forget the fun I had being a part of this theatre's long, magical history. May it continue for another ninety-plus years!"

Opera Southwest

by Tony Zancanella

Tony Zancanella has been the executive director of Opera Southwest since 2012.

The mission of Opera Southwest is to produce quality professional opera enjoyable and accessible to audiences of all ages.

Opera Southwest's folklore includes the story of one of their 1972 founders. Kurt Frederick was a German conductor who stopped in Albuquerque on his way to New York City. His car broke down in Albuquerque and he never left. Kurt was the conductor and music director for seven seasons.

Zancanella continues, "We have produced over 120 major operas at the KiMo for hundreds of thousands of patrons, and we are especially proud to have mounted twenty-three world premieres by local composers, including original operas created especially for Albuquerque's children. These smaller operas stress community and educational themes, and have delighted more than 180,000 youngsters with dazzling, exciting, live theatre. In this way, Opera Southwest ensures a loyal following in future years as these children grow into adulthood. Opera Southwest's outreach programs provide an invaluable service by developing free or very low-cost presentations for school children and underserved individuals or groups. OSW knows that music education not only enriches the lives of everyone, but also markedly improves children's academic performance.

Opera Southwest has staged multiple world premieres of new operas, most of them by New Mexico composers like James Galloway, Alan Stringer, and Robert Tate. Galloway and Sue Ann Gunn were commissioned to write an original opera. The music was recognizable to the kids. Ethan Greene's award-winning *A Way Home* premiered in its revised and orchestrated version at Opera Southwest.

On March 27, 2011, Opera Southwest presented *La traviata* at the KiMo directed by David Bartholomew. It was the last production at the KiMo Theatre for Opera Southwest. For over 30 years, the KiMo Theatre had been the Opera Southwest's home. It moved to the National Hispanic Cultural Center, where, among other continuing production considerations, was the "size of the pit and the restrictions on the orchestra. We sometimes have forty or more musicians to accommodate," Zancanella said.

About the paranormal at the KiMo, Zancanella said, "Bobby? Technical staff and the performers take the paranormal seriously. The theatre people take this Bobby story seriously. We treat ghosts with respect."

La traviata poster. Opera Southwest. Circa 2011.
Courtesy: Opera Southwest.

Books, Film, and Fame

By Jacqueline Murray Loring

In 2019, the KiMo no longer presents first-run movies as it did in the 1920s and 1930s, though it does occasionally host movie premieres. In 2019, it supports Albuquerque's vibrant, evolving independent and local film industry by working with and supporting local film festivals and filmmakers. The KiMo premieres short and independent films made by local filmmakers as part of several film competitions and festivals.

Early in the new century, the State of New Mexico encouraged national and international filmmakers to make movies in New Mexico through its New Mexico Film Office. The Film Office uses the KiMo Theatre's 650 seat Performing Arts Center once or twice a year to host cast, crew, and vendors at movie screenings.

According to Rochelle Bussey, New Mexico Film Office, "We have 250 to 300 people attend events at the KiMo Theatre. Ages 13 and up. These are always considered a major event for local crews in the film and television industry. It is a 'give back' to the locals for all of their hard work on the movie productions." Bussey adds, "Why chose the KiMo? Local theatre, great location, and staff."

According to the website for the Albuquerque Film Office, "The City of Albuquerque's Film Office offers free, dependable assistance to filmmakers. The ABQ Film Office acts as a liaison with City agencies and assists in obtaining locations, equipment, and hotel accommodations for film companies and individuals.

Albuquerque has experienced above the line and below the line crews, talent, and a mix of diverse locations readily available." For years, Albuquerque Film Office Liaison Ann Lerner has worked with the KiMo Theatre to sponsor, support, and showcase local short and independent films.

The Duke City Shootout

By Anthony DellaFlora, Filmmaker

The KiMo Theatre offers local screenwriters, actors, filmmakers, and their crews the opportunity and a place to showcase their films. The Duke City Shootout, Indie Q, 48 Hour Film Project, Albuquerque Film and Music Event, and the University of New Mexico's filmmakers are among the artists who have found a home at the KiMo where they can gather with friends and watch their films on the silver screen.

Flicks on 66 was the first filmmaking festival launched in 2000 in Albuquerque. The format was simple. After scripts were chosen through an intensive selection process, the writers were brought to Albuquerque from all over the United States, and given one week to shoot, edit, and premiere their short films with crews and equipment supplied by the festival. The KiMo Theatre drew a full house for the film screenings and awards ceremony the second year of the festival on July 21, 2001. Albuquerque Mayor Jim Baca was among the attendees and gave out the award for best picture, known as the Palm de Grease. The annual event, which eventually changed its name to the Duke City Shootout, continued until 2010 (with a break in 2009). The festival, founded by Jim Graebner, Anthony DellaFlora, Dennis Gromelski, and Steve Anderson, produced more than seventy short films over ten festivals."

Indie Q at the KiMo

Over the course of the year, the KiMo hosts several film festivals. "Indie Q is Albuquerque's independent film community in action. According to Ann Lerner, founder and organizer of the film showings, "It is composed of local actors, producers, animators, screenwriters, directors, and general fans of film and hosts a film festival quarterly at the KiMo Theatre."

The 48 Hour Film Project

The 48 Hour Film Project

The 48 Hour Film Project is a yearly, "wild and sleepless weekend" in which teams make a movie in just 48 hours. This international film project, founded in 2001 by Albuquerque's Mark Ruppert and Liz Langston, "challenges filmmakers and crews to write, film, add music, edit, and submit a short film within forty-eight hours." The brainchild of Ruppert and Langston, the film project is now a national and international contest. The national website claims "over 30,000 films have been made since 2001". All films produced by local artists over a July weekend are shown at the KiMo Theatre the week after the project finishes. The movies are judged by the audience. The best ten films are shown at the KiMo the following week. Local winners go on to represent Albuquerque in the national contest. The international and national winners show their films at the Cannes Film Festival Short Film Corner. In 2017, the KiMo Theatre did not host the 48 Hour Film Project due to restorations and addition of new carpeting throughout the theatre.

Albuquerque Film & Media Experience

The KiMo is among several theaters that host the Albuquerque Film & Music Experience. Liz Langston is the founder, and in 2017, Ivan Wiener and Kendra Crooks were the producers. According to the website, the AFME is "Albuquerque's premier film and music festival now in its sixth year."

Animal Humane at the KiMo

June 2018 is the fourth anniversary of the Animal Humane New Mexico and Albuquerque Film Office's partnership to produce the Annual Feline Film Festival. The 2017 screening of feline films theme was "The Good, the Bad and the Cuddly". In 2015 at their first festival, over 300 cat and film lovers watched the best films from the new film competition. Many of the films were directed by New Mexico filmmakers. Their website declares: "We are excited to bring this paw-pular event to Albuquerque's historical KiMo Theatre as it continues to grow!"

Marquee. Feline Film Festival. Circa 2017.
Courtesy: Brad Stoddard.
New Mexico Post Alliance

The Post Alliance

Brad Stoddard, president, New Mexico Post Alliance, said, "We have used the KiMo for New Mexico Post Alliance membership events at least six times over four years. Our audience can range in age from sixteen to ninety-six. We chose the KiMo over other venues because of its ambiance, screen size, and sound system. Also, it's downtown and has a lobby for an art gallery. Everyone loves the art deco theatre. The KiMo is uniquely New Mexico and one of the most beautiful historical theatres on Route 66. It is always a pleasure to sit in the cushy seats and look up at the great beamed ceiling and steer heads with glowing red eyes surrounding the stage."

The KiMo, Movies, Television, and Movie Stars

The KiMo has had its own share of fame as celebrities visited and performed on its stage. Every year the theatre hosts internationally known speakers, poets, and authors from Ginger Rogers to Bryan Cranston to Kevin Eubanks, who played in concert as part of the Jazz Workshop's 40th Birthday Celebration 2016. Eubanks is a jazz guitarist and composer known for his appearance on *The Tonight Show with Jay Leno*.

Breaking Bad

According to Larry Parker, Bryan Cranston and the crew and cast of hit television series *Breaking Bad* gathered at the KiMo. Speaking to the crew from the stage, Cranston laughed that on the program his character had just escaped from his hospital bed, interrupting his chemotherapy treatment and "here I am at the KiMo." Parker remembers those in the audience thought that was funny. Parker said later he saw the show Cranston mentioned and for a quick moment, Walter White rode on a bus by the KiMo sign. "You had to look quick, but there we were."

During the shooting years and after, the *Breaking Bad* crew and cast were no strangers to the KiMo. As a way of saying thank you to the folks of Albuquerque for his positive experience during the six years while he produced *Breaking Bad*, Stewart Lyons gave a free talk about the movie industry at the KiMo in April 2013.

In October 2016, Bryan Cranston stopped at the KiMo on his book tour to discuss to a sellout crowd his memoir, *A Life in Parts*. Bob Odenkirk (*Breaking Bad*'s Saul Goodman) and Bryan Cranston (*Breaking Bad*'s Walter White) were reunited onstage for an evening titled "A Word with Writers."

In a 2017 episode of *Better Call Saul*, a spin-off from *Breaking Bad*, viewers saw Chuck McGill (played by Michael McKean), the brother of Jimmy McGill (played by Bob Odenkirk), shuffling down Central Avenue past the KiMo Theatre, wrapped in his quirky foil protection.

In 2017, Steven Michael Quezada was in his first term as a Bernalillo County, (Albuquerque) Commissioner for District 2. He has a long record of public service for the county but he is better recognized as a Screen Actors Guild award-winning actor, producer, and comedian, as well as DEA Agent Steven Gomez on the Emmy Award-winning television series *Breaking Bad*. Quezada proudly admits the KiMo is "where he started his acting career." "The KiMo is where I started my career. The energy of the artists who performed there somehow remains. So many performers' dreams started at the KiMo. If only the walls could talk, the stories we would hear. The KiMo will always be in my heart."

The KiMo is a Movie Star

The KiMo Theatre itself has appeared in several movies and has hosted many premiers of movies shot in New Mexico or written or produced by residents of New Mexico or Albuquerque.

In 2011, a Disney Channel Original musical movie, *Lemonade Mouth*, was partially filmed in the KiMo, and the theatre has been a backdrop in several other films and television series, including *In Plain Sight* and *Better Call Saul*.

Full length feature movies filmed in New Mexico are frequently premiered at the KiMo. In 2007, *Wild Hogs*, about four men reaching midlife crisis who head for the open road on their motorcycles, premiered at the KiMo. *Wild Hogs* was directed by Walt Becher and starred Tim Allen, Martin Lawrence, William H. Macy, and John Travolta. It was filmed on the roads of New Mexico and in the village of Madrid.

Other films premiered at the KiMo include *Frank* (2014), starring Maggie Gyllenhaal and Michael Fassbender and directed by Lenny Abrahamson and shot in Dublin and New Mexico; *Gold* (2016), directed by Stephen Gaghan and starring Matthew McConaughey, Edgar Ramirez, and Bryce Dallas Howard; and *The Space Between Us* (2017), directed by Peter Chelsom and starring Gary Oldman, Asa Butterfield, and Carla Gugino.

50 to 1, the story about the New Mexican horse, Mine That Bird, which won the 2009 Kentucky Derby, was partially filmed in New Mexico. It was directed by Jim Wilson and starred Skeet Ulrich, Christian Kane, and William Devane, with Albuquerque residents Michael and Trish Miller. It premiered on March 19, 2014, at the KiMo.

In 2016, *The Lost Pueblo* premiered at the KiMo. Tomas Sanchez, an Albuquerque native and filmmaker, directed the film, which was produced in 2016 in New Mexico with ninety-five percent of the cast and crew from this state.

Book Cover. *The Fall and Rise of Champagne Sanchez.* Courtesy: Rudy Miera. Circa 2017.

Photo credit: Rudy Miera.

Books Featuring the KiMo

Though the KiMo has never been the subject of its own book (until now!), it is featured in dozens of nonfiction and fiction books.

Nonfiction books include

Pueblo Deco by Carla Breeze. Paperback. Publisher: Rizzoli (1990). ISBN-13: 978-0847811779;

Albuquerque Then and Now by Mo Palmer. Hardcover. Publisher: Thunder Bay Press (2006). ISBN-13: 978- 1592236558;

Albuquerque Deco and Pueblo (Images of America) by Paul R. Secord. Paperback; Series of America. Arcadia Publishing (2012). ISBN-13: 978-0738595269;

KiMo King of Its Kind (Grand Opening Book 1) Kindle Edition by Christine Morrelli. Amazon Digital Services LLC (2012). ASIN: B009B8Y0N0.

Legendary Locals of Albuquerque by Richard Melzer. Paperback. Legendary Locals. Arcadia Publishing (2015). ISBN-13:978-1467101974.

Two recent novels written by SouthWest Writers members predominantly feature the KiMo Theatre:

The Fall and Rise of Champagne Sanchez by Rudy Miera. Paperback. CreateSpace Independent Publishing Platform (2016). ISBN-13: 978-1539869160

The Detectives Who Loved Opera by Babs (Barbara) Langner. Paperback. Publisher: CreateSpace Independent Publishing Platform (2013). ISBN-13: 978-1484169049.

"*The Fall and Rise of Champagne Sanchez* follows Santos and his cousin, Adelita, as they live and learn from their struggles that take place in the Albuquerque barrios, Old Town the UNM campus, and reach a triumphant peak in a day of community unity in the historic KiMo Theatre. Adelita's reflections of their follies, tragedies, and miracles are detailed in her 'Journal Entries' interspersed throughout the comic novel."

The Detectives Who Loved Opera web site states, "Mysterious happenings at the KiMo Theatre frighten the cast members rehearsing the opera *Carmen*. When the chandelier crashes to the floor, a seer blames a ghost. The journalists pick up on this reference and tell their readers a phantom of the opera exists in Albuquerque. Murder backstage escalates the situation. As a result, the box office thrives when every performance sells out. *Carmen* at the KiMo is a hit."

For more information on organizations, groups, and events in this section, see the following links:

National League of American Pen Women: http://www.nlapw.org/

KiMo art gallery submissions: https://www.cabq.gov/culturalservices/kimo/art-gallery- submissions

Ballet Repertory Theatre of New Mexico: www.brtnm.com

Albuquerque concert promoters: http://www.ampconcerts.org and http://www.launchpadrocks.com/

Public art in Albuquerque: http://www.cabq.gov/culturalservices/public-art

KiMo sign replacement project: https://www.abqjournal.com/40933/kimo-sign-emphasizes- artistic.html and David Steinberg's article in the *Albuquerque Journal* on July 3, 2011

June 3, 2011, sign dedication gala: https://www.cabq.gov/culturalservices/public- art/events/dedication-of-the-kimo-theatres-new-neon-sign

Alloy Orchestra: http://www.alloyorchestra.com/ New Mexico Philharmonic: http://www.nmphil.org
Mayor Berry's press release: http://www.cabq.gov/mayor/news/mayor-berry-reveals-new- 2018silver-screen2019-at-kimo-theatre

American Institute of Architects Albuquerque: http://www.aiaabq.org/
Fractal Foundation: http://fractalfoundation.org/
Organization of Competitive Bodybuilders: http://www.thenaturalmusclenetwork.com
New Mexico Young Actors: http://www.nmyoungactors.org/#Home
New Mexico Film Office: http://www.nmfilm.com

City of Albuquerque Film Office: https://www.cabq.gov/economicdevelopment/film Indie Q: http://indieq.ning.com/
48 Hour Film Project: http://www.48hourfilm.com/home Albuquerque Film and Music Experience: https://www.abqfilmx.com/
Annual Feline Film Festival:

http://www.kimotickets.com/event/279745/3rd-annual-feline-film- festival-the-good-the-bad-amp-the-cuddly

For a fun discussion of horror films by Larry Parker and Anthony DellaFlora, see https://www.youtube.com/watch?v=tqA88f3veyk&t=689s

SouthWest Writers   www.southwestwriters.com

Albuquerque Plans the Theatre's 90th Anniversary Celebration

The Planning Committee

The 2017 KiMo Theatre planning committee stayed true to the history and spirit of the theatre when they planned the KiMo's year-long celebration of events and performances. Whether you were a fan of music, spoken word, dance, theatre, or film from January to December 2017, there was an event for you to enjoy at the KiMo.

The Mayor's Office

In 2017, the Mayor's Office and the City of Albuquerque's Cultural Services Department oversaw the long list of City rental properties. The list includes many of Albuquerque's favorite places including the New Mexico Veteran's Memorial on Louisiana Boulevard, the Old Town Gazebo in Old Town and the Albuquerque Museum on Mountain Road, as well as two city-owned theatres: one at the South Broadway Cultural Center on Broadway Boulevard and the KiMo Theatre on Central Avenue. The KiMo Theatre can be rented by groups, organizations, and for private functions.

Albuquerque's Cultural Services Department

The KiMo Theatre's 90th anniversary events for 2017 were overseen by Cultural Services Director, Dana Feldman and Deputy Director Dave Mathews.

The Community Event Manager oversees the Events Planning Division. This department is managed by Nikki Peone who is responsible for many of the city's event rentals. Peone and Larry Parker and his staff:

Events Coordinator, Chris Meloy, Technical Manager Mark Ferris and manager for the box office, Michelle King were primarily responsible for the events and performances enjoyed by the community during the KiMo's anniversary year.

Larry Parker was master of ceremonies for the anniversary events including the celebration party on September 16th when he introduced the silent, black and white film *The General* staring Buster Keaton which featured music performed live on-stage by the Alloy Orchestra. The movie showed to a packed house.

Event Planning

According to Community Events Manager Peone, an event of the magnitude of the KiMo's year- long celebration had to be coordinated with dozens of KiMo supporters. Ann Lerner, the City of Albuquerque's Office of Economic Development Department Film Office Liaison was "essential to the planning," Peone said. The plan for 2017 was to excite and interest both residents, tourists and visitors of all ages.

Among the 2017 celebration planners were Mayor Richard J. Berry, his office staff including Rhiannon Samuel, Director of Communications, the staff in the Cultural Services Department and the Events Planning Division, along with assistance from the city's marketing specialist, Tanya Lenti and marketing consultant, Marti Wolfe

A whole year of celebrating the 90th anniversary required the cooperation of KiMo supporters including city departments, community leaders, groups, businesses, organizations, and individuals. Peone said, "Of course, you can't have a celebration without the support of thousands of audience members who attended the scheduled events."

"We want folks to come back Downtown, and we want folks to come to the KiMo," said Cultural Services Director, Dana Feldman. "I think the restorations and our new program changes are really in step with each other. We have all kinds of programing to offer at the KiMo."

Music, Movies and More

During the year-long celebration, the KiMo kept its doors open for groups and individuals wishing to rent the facility and provide programs along with the 90th anniversary events arranged specifically by the planning committee. In 2017, audiences were entertained by a diverse schedule including silent films, a horror film festival, Pueblo Indian drumming, and dancing, traditional mariachi, flamenco, and New Mexican folk music. Tarde de Oro celebrated the culture of New Mexico and the American Southwest presented by the City Office of Senior Affairs.

The 90th Anniversary Celebration

The list of anniversary events, most of which were free and open to the public included:

90th Anniversary Signature Book Event-Bookworks and Live at the KiMo presented readings and book signings with: Douglas Preston, *The Lost City of the Monkey God: A True Story*; C. J. Box with *Vicious Circles*; and Anne Hillerman with *Song of the Lion*.

Past book signings include author and actor Bryan Cranston; internationally renowned Chilean-American author Isabel Allende; British writer and Emeritus Professor of Medical Law at the University of Edinburgh Alexander McCall Smith; and Michael Wallis, historian, voice of the movie Cars.

Chautauqua Presentations

The New Mexico Humanities Council and the New Mexico Department of Cultural Affairs presented four monthly programs. February featured Chautauqua with Ms. Brenda Hollingsworth-Marley as Billie Holiday to celebrate Black History Month. In March, Chautauqua Dr. Steve Cormier with Music from the Ranch and the Open Range. April showcased Chautauqua Dr. Cipriano Vigil and Family who presented Traditional New Mexican Folk Music. Chautauqua Consuelo Luz presented Sephardic Jews in New Mexico–Stories and Songs in June.

Movies and History

During 2017, the KiMo presented as their Signature Events films based on books that won the Pulitzer Prize. The films included *The Magnificent Andersons* (1942), *All the King's Men* (1949), *The Old Man and the Sea* (1958), *To Kill a Mockingbird* (1962), *The Age of Innocence* (1993), *Ben-Hur* (1959), *The Hours* (2003), and *The Road* (2009).

The KiMo presented on September 16, 2017, Buster Keaton in *The General* (1926) with the Alloy Orchestra who performed its original score to this silent comic classic. October featured a Halloween Weekend Horror Film Festival: A Tribute to Boris Karloff. The anniversary year ended with a film festival for the entire family. The KiMo presented all eight Harry Potter films.

Poetry Party

The headline for the flyer for an event at the KiMo on September 22, 2017 reads, "Albuquerque Poetry Party: A Showcase of ABQ Celebrated Poets" The flyer continues, "Open without charge to the community, on Friday evening September 22, 2017, the KiMo Theatre will host a "poetry party" featuring a dozen award-winning poets who make Albuquerque their home. Jessica Helen Lopez, the City of Albuquerque's Second Poet Laureate (2014 to 2016) will serve as the evening's Master of Ceremonies."

Steven Toya and Native Drumming and Dance
Southern Slam Dance Group. Circa 2017.
Courtesy: Steven Toya Sr.

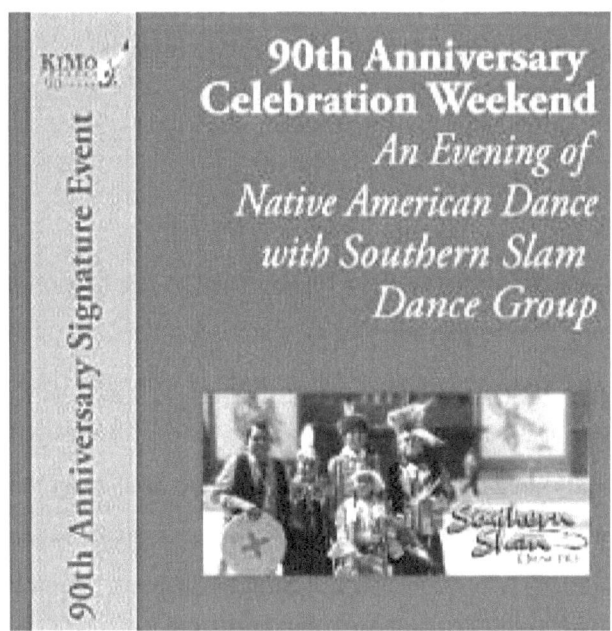

Southern Slam Dance Group. Announcement "An Evening of Native American Dance with Southern Slam Dance Group at KiMo Theatre." Circa 2017. Courtesy: KiMo Theatre and Steven Toya Sr.

According to the KiMo Theatre's web site, the September 23, 2017 performance event featured, "An Evening of Native American Dance: with Southern Slam Dance Group."

The web site continued, "On Saturday evening, September 23rd, 2017, the KiMo Theatre in Downtown Albuquerque will present the award-winning and internationally renowned Southern Slam Dance Group from Albuquerque's nearby Zia Pueblo. Southern Slam was honored as the only New Mexico drum group invited to help host the Gathering of Nations Pow Wow in Albuquerque in April 2017. Southern Slam was a top-contender and prizewinner in the Pow Wow's Southern Singing Challenge this year."

A special feature of the September 23rd evening's program was ceremonial drumming and blessings songs recognizing and honoring the KiMo Theatre's entertainment history since 1927, and its current status as a city, state, and national landmark. The KiMo Theatre is one of the few remaining theatres in the American Southwest built and now carefully restored in the Pueblo Deco style that celebrates American Indian symbols and design motifs.

Steven Toya Sr. is a flutist, lead singer, and founder of the Southern Slam Dance Group. This select group from Albuquerque's nearby Zia Pueblo hosts over a dozen drummers, singers, and dancers from Toya's extended Pueblo family. The two-part 90-minute program was designed for families and audiences of all ages. The admission to this celebration was free to the public.

According to Toya, "Ceremonial blessing songs and prayers were a significant feature of the grand opening festivities at the KiMo Theatre on

September 19th, 1927. Southern Slam will drum and recite sacred prayers at their KiMo performance asking for the continued preservation and programming success of one of New Mexico's most distinguished landmark theatres.

We do traditional dancing which consists of the Plains style of the Comanche and we do the traditional style of dancing which consists of Hopi style and the traditional Pueblo. What I mean by traditional dance is we don't do ceremonial dances. We don't wear the traditional paints covering our bodies. We might do a little paint on our faces but that's where I separate the ceremonial from the traditional. When I say traditional dance, it will be in traditional regalia without the ceremonial paints."

The performers themselves ranged in age from two-year-old Loloma Toya to the 84-year-old tribal elder, Ada Toya. Traditional and contemporary Native American dances included the Rainbow Dance, featuring Todd Toya, aged 27, and Jowanna Toya, aged 15; and the Eagle Dance, featuring Steven Toya, Jr., aged 28, and Kyle Toya, aged 17. Other performances included the Women's Buckskin and Southern Cloth Dance and the Fancy Shawl Dance and Girl's jingle Dress Dance. Toys said, "We do a lot of social dancing where I try to include the audiences. What we're doing is giving thanks. Like my late father told me, "When you do a show, include the people, whether they are Native American or not." What we are doing is giving thanks because life is precious." Toya continued, "When I do our shows, I try to be the most respectful to all nationalities, all colors of peoples. My goal is to send everyone home with good feeling of sharing, a blessing, so we can learn to respect all people's cultures.

Before we do our performances, we honor the flag of glory, the red, white and blue. After we honor the flag of glory to be proud Americans, our next song is to honor our veterans with a veteran's song. We always honor all our warrior people. We always give them thanks. They are a part of our warrior prayers. We sing an important song called the Memorial Song it to honor each and every one of our identities. We are part of the Family Tree. After those three important songs, we do our performance with the live entertainment.

The blessing comes with every song whether it comes with the Veteran song or the Flag song or the song for the elderly or the new born. Every song we sing has a meaning to it. We don't sing just to sing. We do have some harmony songs but the majority of our songs we do have a purpose, a reason and blessings always follow because we are using the most powerful instrument known to man. It is called the heartbeat of the drum. If you utilize these instruments, the drum, the rattle, the flute, the bells, a lot of miracle healings can be done."

KiMo Theatre: Fact and Folklore

SECTION III

The Tour of the KiMo Theatre

KiMo Theatre. Circa 2017. Photo credit: Alexandra Dell'Amore.

Marquee. Neon sign. Ticket office. Circa 2017.
Photo credit: Alexandra Dell'Amore.

The Grand Exterior

By Jacqueline Murray Loring

The Marquee

In 2017, the KiMo Theatre at 423 Central Avenue, Route 66, Albuquerque, New Mexico celebrated its 90th anniversary. The theatre is a national treasure and a unique tourist attraction that is open to both guided and self-guided tours during regular business hours. The KiMo Theatre's ticket office is at the corner of Central Avenue and Fifth Street west of the theatre's main entrance.

Marquee. Macbeth. Circa 2013. Photo credit: Brad Stoddard.

KiMo Manager Larry Parker said he frequently gives tours of the theatre and often hears heart-warming tales from the past. Tourists and locals recall enjoying silent films or watching the early, first-run talkies shown at the KiMo. A son remembered a family story about his mother playing castanets along with the organist during a 1930s silent film. Parker recalls an older man who detailed a first date at the KiMo when he was a teenager. A woman told of a stolen kiss in the balcony. There are remembrances of a horror movie scream, the jubilation of watching Pueblo or Ehecatl dancers, and an artist's pride at seeing her painting hung in the art gallery by the popcorn stand.

When you plan to visit, it is best to call ahead to check if the theatre is open for tours. The theatre lobby and auditorium may be closed to the public during daytime rehearsals for evening events and during scheduled activities.

If you find yourself in the neighborhood, don't be afraid to walk into the ticket office lobby and ask about a guided tour. If that tour isn't available, ask to tour the theatre on your own. If the theatre is booked for an event and unavailable for touring, the renovated [2017] ticket office lobby is also adorned with classic movie posters, old photographs, and KiMo Theatre memorabilia, It offers a fascinating look into the history of the theatre. The lobby is also your chance to meet Mr. and Mrs. Bachechi Their portraits hang on the lobby wall.

The theatre is open Wednesday through Saturday from 11 a.m. to 8 p.m. and on Sunday from 11 a.m. to 3 p.m. The KiMo is closed on Mondays, Tuesdays and City holidays. Guided tours are limited by the availability of tour guides and are arranged by appointment only. For more information about KiMo tours, call (505) 768-3544 or email: kimotheatre@cabq.gov during business hours.

Knowledge of the history of the KiMo Theatre, an understanding of its design, construction, and native influences, how it was named, and an appreciation of the depth of the investment in the KiMo the Albuquerque community has made over ninety years will enhance your visit and your tour.

KiMo Theatre: Fact and Folklore is a handy guide to take with you as you tour the outside and inside of the KiMo building. Contributors to this book have shared with you important and interesting historical facts, points of interest, fun antidotes, and some secrets. After your tour, share your KiMo story with the staff, and be sure to sign the KiMo Theatre and the City of Albuquerque's Guest Book before you leave.

Oreste Bachechi and Carl Boller traveled throughout New Mexico, visiting the pueblos of Acoma and Isleta, and the Navajo Nation. After months of research, Carl Boller submitted a watercolor rendering for the theatre that pleased Oreste Bachechi. The interior was to include plaster ceiling beams textured to look like logs and painted with dance and hunt scenes, air vents disguised as Navajo rugs, chandeliers shaped like war drums and Native American funeral canoes, wrought iron birds descending the stairs and rows of garlanded buffalo skulls with eerie, glowing amber eyes.

None of the designs were chosen at random. Each of the myriad images of rain clouds, birds and swastikas had historical significance. The Navajo swastika is a symbol for life, freedom and happiness.

Like its abstract symbols, color, too, was part of the Indian vocabulary. Yellow represents the life-giving sun, white the approaching morning, red the setting sun of the West and black the darkening clouds from the North. The crowning touch was the nine large wall murals painted in oil by Carl Von Hassler. Working from 20-foot-high scaffolding, Von Hassler spent months on his creations.*

The section above is used with permission from:
https://www.cabq.gov/culturalservices/kimo/about-the-theatre.
Edited by John Arnold, New Mexico Museum of Natural History,
with information provided by the KiMo Theatre.

KiMo Theatre foyer. Circa 1927. Courtesy: Albuquerque Museum.

Construction Influences

The KiMo Theatre Tour begins with construction influences in 1927. Native American art provided inspiration for the KiMo design and construction, especially the Acoma, Isleta, and Navajo artwork.

Auditorium. Side wall swastikas. Circa 1980s.
Courtesy of Rush Dudley.

Redeeming Swastikas

by Sam Moorman
Author and SouthWest Writers Member

I was shocked during my first visit to the KiMo Theatre in Albuquerque to see large swastikas framing the stage like wall art. "How do they get away with that?" I wondered, coming from politically correct California, where such displays would prompt sign-waving protests.

Again, during my 2010 tour of Japan, I was amazed to see swastikas boldly stamped all over city maps. But this only shows my early ignorance of a symbol that is revered today and was in ancient times among cultures worldwide. On Japanese maps, it spots Buddhist temples. In the KiMo Theatre, it fits the Native American tribal design.

The core of the ancient swastika is a mathematical plus sign, or equal-armed, upright cross. On my Japan map, each cross end was bent ninety degrees to the left, or counterclockwise. The World War II symbol had its cross ends always bent to the right, or clockwise. I relied on this distinction until I saw some ancient swastikas with ends bent right also.

The real difference between the World War II emblem and the original swastika is that Nazis rotated the original symbol forty-five degrees, converting its upright plus sign to an X. This also tilted the bent ends so the altered symbol seems to balance on one point. The variant can look like arms and legs of a sprinting stick figure with one shoe tip touching ground.

Auditorium. Ceiling swastikas. Circa 1927.
Courtesy: Albuquerque Museum.

The ancient, respected swastika maintains at its core a vertical plus sign. The end extensions, whether bent left or right, allow the true swastika to rest solidly on one flat, level base. The entire symbol can seem like a stick figure kneeling on one knee, with two arms flung upward in praise.

The sullied Nazi emblem with its X tilt (and link to horrid pogroms) should not even be called a swastika. It's a bastard offshoot of the respected symbol that decorates the KiMo Theatre and Japanese maps. Once the Nazi sign is correctly identified it should simply be called that, or some coined name like Nazika (Nahtsika). Any wordsmith would likely agree that the definition of swastika, like Shakespeare's love, is not true "which alters when it alteration finds."

Knowing this, I no longer cringe when I see true swastikas. I like that they are boldly shown in the KiMo Theatre and on Japanese maps. They defy the stigma of the variant, and lead people like me to learn the meaning of the original symbol. This is basic education, part of the ongoing struggle between knowledge and ignorance.

Native American Influences
by Kathy Wagoner

Native American culture influenced not only the KiMo's architecture and name but its interior design. Images from nature adorn the outside and inside of the building as do other symbols of significance to Indian culture at the time the building was constructed in 1927, including the Navajo "whirling log," an ancient symbol for life, peace, and prosperity.

Color also plays an important part in symbolizing the natural elements of our world. In addition to many unique decorations, such as the buffalo skulls with glowing amber eyes near the ceilings and wrought iron birds along the staircase, Von Hassler's nine large 'Seven Cities of Cibola' murals depict pueblos and ruins that still exist in the Southwest."

According to information archived at the University of New Mexico's Center for Southwest Research and Special Collections, the KiMo Theatre was built to rival theatres worldwide. Many of the photographs in the Nicholas P. Ciotola Italians in Albuquerque Pictorial Collection in the Center for Southwest Research and Special Collections were taken in the mid-1920s.

> *"The Kimo Theatre, which opened in September of 1927, was perhaps the most unique Italian-owned business in Albuquerque. Financed by Italian immigrant Oreste Bachechi and envisioned by Maria Bachechi, the Kimo Theatre's Native American theme was meant to rival the far eastern and Moorish theatres that were becoming popular at the time in Los Angeles and other world cities."*

Courtesy of Nicholas P. Ciotola.)
https://nmstatehood.unm.edu/search/node/KiMo%20theatre
Collection: Nicholas P. Ciotola Italians in Albuquerque
Pictorial Collection Title: Postcard of the Kimo Theatre, ca.
1927 Creator: Ciotola, Nicholas P.
Subject: Italian Americans; Albuquerque (N.M.)-History; Business enterprises-New Mexico- Albuquerque; Albuquerque (N.M.)-Theatres; KiMo Theatre (Albuquerque, N.M.)

For more information:
https://www.britannica.com/topic/Seven-Cities-of-Cibola

KiMo Theatre foyer. Circa 2017.

Photo credit: Alexandra Dell'Amore.

KiMo Theatre foyer. Ticket booth. Circa 2017.
Photo credit: Alexandra Dell'Amore.

KiMo Theatre. Central Avenue and Fifth Street. Window trim. Circa 1990s. Courtesy: KiMo Theatre.

Starting Your Walking Tour

By Jacqueline Murray Loring

This book begins its tour outside the three story, iconic, and historic KiMo Theatre building on Central Avenue in the exterior lobby. Here you will discover the main theatre doors, the ticket booth, distinctive tiles, and movie posters. Follow the Pueblo-Deco motif as it wraps west around the building past the KiMo Theatre Ticket Office at 421 Central Avenue to the corner at Fifth Street. Above you are the theatre's windows with their colorful and decorative window trim. From this corner, you can look back at the theatre's marquee and newly renovated KiMo neon sign.

Marquee. *Steve Earl and the Dukes*. Circa 2017
Photo credit: Alexandra Dell'Amore.

KiMo Theatre. Neon sign. At twilight. Circa 2017.
Photo credit: Brad Stoddard.

Neon Sign Restoration

The KiMo Theatre marquee and neon sign have a history of their own. In ninety years, the theatre, marquee, and sign have been center stage for many of New Mexico and Albuquerque's major celebrations including the city's centennial celebration in 2012 and celebration of its own reopening. The original sign from 1927 was removed sometime before the City of Albuquerque bought the building in 1977. Photographs of the evolution of the KiMo marquee and neon sign can be found in dozens of photographs housed in collections including the one at the Albuquerque Museum and Zimmerman Library.

In 2011, the city agreed to add a replica of the original sign.

"Restoring the twenty-four-foot neon sign to the front of the theatre in 2011 was an important moment for the KiMo and the city," said Parker.

According to Dana Feldman, director in 2017 of the City of Albuquerque's Cultural Services Department, "We had a celebration for the KiMo's 85th anniversary when we installed the new neon sign at the KiMo."

The sign was partially funded through the Urban Enhancement Trust Fund (UETF) which every two years provides funds that enhance and enrich the culture of the City of Albuquerque. Albuquerque's Art in Municipal Places Ordinance sets aside 1% of City construction funds derived from the general obligation bond program and certain revenue bonds for the purchase or commission of works of art.

How complicated is it to fund and add a sign to a city-owned building? A city-owned, national treasure? How many city or national entities have to agree to paint a KiMo wall, restore a mural, install new carpeting, remove every seat in the auditorium, add a crossover aisle or an art gallery, update handicapped bathrooms, set up a bar, or apply for a wine license?

And whom do you go to for the money to do the updating? How complicated is it to request a GO bond (General Obligation bond) from city voters? And get a positive vote? Could there be any other considerations to the decision to replace the KiMo neon sign?

For the discussion in 2010 focused on restored the KiMo marquee, first the design for the new sign needed to be agreed upon by all parties involved in KiMo Theatre decision making. Then there was the issue of the colors of the neon and the sign itself, and where and how to attach it to the historic building. No one knew what the original colors were, because no color photographs of the sign existed.

Nevertheless, the sign had to be as close to the original as folks could imagine, design, and construct. It had to match the exterior decor. And how do you get to it for repairs once it is installed? The task was increasingly more complicated because all renovations, updating, corrections, additions, deletions, demolition and/or construction, and installations are determined by more than a handful of federal, state, city, and community organizations and groups, as well as laws, expectations, pride, and voters.

Because the KiMo is on the National Register of Historic Places and the New Mexico State Register of Cultural Properties—plus it is an Albuquerque Historic Landmark—any and all changes to the KiMo are complicated.

In order to add a square of new carpeting, renovate Carl Von Hassler's murals, or replicate a 1927 neon sign, the city must have agreement from and be in compliance with the National Historic Preservation Act (NHPA; Public Law 89-665; 54 U.S.C. 300101 et seq. created the National Register of Historic Places, the list of National Historic Landmarks, and the State Historic Preservation Offices), New Mexico State Register of Cultural Properties, New Mexico Historic Preservation Division of the New Mexico Department of Cultural Affairs, Americans with Disabilities Act (ADA), Albuquerque City Council, the Mayor's Office, and the Landmarks and Urban Conservation Commission of the City of Albuquerque.

In the case of the KiMo's marquee, those involved also included but weren't limited to the Albuquerque Arts Board, Zeon Signs, and folks like Ed Boles, the city's historic preservation planner; Craig Rivera, manager of the city's Community Events Division; Betty Rivera, head of the city's Cultural Services Department; and Johnnie Meier, past president of the New Mexico Route 66 Association. And who would pay for the sign? The voters of Albuquerque and the good-hearted folks at the Urban Enhancement Trust Fund Division came forward to pay for the renovations.

According to Matthew Carter, Project Planner with the Public Art Urban Enhancement Division, City of Albuquerque Cultural Services Department, "In 2011, the Public Art Program was approached by then-City Historian Ed Boles (retired) from the City Planning Department and Larry Parker from the KiMo Theatre.

A request was made to the Arts Board for consideration of recreating and funding a new neon sign on the side of the historic KiMo Theatre. It was determined by the Arts Board and staff that this was a special onetime request for the Public Art Program to use one percent funds to recreate a historic sign.

One percent funds are not generally allowed to be used for signs. It is our understanding that Zeon Signs, a local neon sign company that built the original sign, worked with historic images and discovered of some of the original blueprints. Because the sign had to be redesigned and reconstructed from scratch by sign artists, it was approved by the Arts Board with full endorsement by Mayor Berry."

On June 3, 2011, Mayor Richard Berry invited the community to a gala evening celebration for the dedication of the historic sign. The ceremony, dedication, and lighting were followed by a screening of Fritz Lang's 1927 masterpiece *Metropolis*. The classic silent film had been fully restored in HD with twenty-five minutes of lost footage.

The Alloy Orchestra from Massachusetts performed an original score. The Alloy Orchestra is a three-man musical ensemble who write and perform live accompaniment to classic silent films. According to their web site, "They work with an outrageous assemblage of peculiar objects; they thrash and grind soulful music from unlikely sources."

Photos of the dedication, both day shots and brilliant evening pictures of the neon sign, can be enjoyed at the KiMo, the Albuquerque Museum, the *Albuquerque Journal,* and the University of New Mexico. Among the pictures are many of the 1920s and 1930s antique cars that lined Central Avenue, Route 66.

According to Larry Parker, "Putting the new neon sign back on the building was important. It said to people the KiMo is back. It redefines this corner of Central Avenue. The funds for the 24-foot sign came from a general obligation bond for half a million dollars approved by voters in 2009. That money was also used for a new air conditioning system in the auditorium, equipment upgrades such as a sound board and HD projector, and to clean, repair and paint the exterior stucco, among other things."

Inside the Ticket Office Lobby

The KiMo Theatre's ticket office at the corner of Central Avenue and Fifth Street, west of the theatre's main entrance, is filled with historical photographs, memorabilia, and posters. Some of the photographs were taken over the years by KiMo Theatre staff but many are copies of pictures that belong to museums, libraries, and personal collections. Over ninety years, the names of some of those photographed or the name of the photographer for these historic pictures have been lost.

The KiMo Theatre photo archive at the University of New Mexico's Zimmerman Library was an official project of the New Mexico State Centennial and funded by the University of New Mexico Libraries and the Center for Regional Studies. The archive holds pictures that document events at the KiMo as well as pictures of famous people and Hollywood stars who have visited the KiMo including Ginger Rogers, Sally Rand, Gloria Swanson, Tom Mix and silent film cowboy Buck Jones who went on to sign with Columbia Pictures to do talkies. One photograph in their collection shows Maria Bachechi pinning a corsage on Ginger Rogers. A copy of that historical KiMo theatre photograph can also be seen among dozens of others in the KiMo ticket office.

- https://nmstatehood.unm.edu/search/node/KiMo%20theatre.
- https://www.cabq.gov/culturalservices/public-art/about-public-art-1

Façade. America's Foremost Indian Theatre. Announcement "Sally Rand in her fan and bubble dances". Circa 1930s. Courtesy: Albuquerque Museum.

Sally Rand at the KiMo

Oreste Bachechi must have believed that over the years his movie palace would continue to show silent films and provide a stage for vaudeville and burlesque. Film in its early days was considered a fad that would not last. But by the time Mr. Bachechi died, vaudeville, popular since the 1880s, was seeing its audiences dwindle.

Burlesque, popular since the 1860s, held on till the 1940s, but by the late 1920s, both art forms moved out of theatres into bars and social clubs. In 1927, though, vaudeville and out of town road shows shared the stage at the KiMo with silent films.

Sally Rand, one of the most famous burlesque dancers, played the KiMo in 1936. Rand was known for her ostrich feather fan dance. She was one of the last vaudeville performers to perform at the KiMo.

A photograph of the marque on the KiMo during one of Rand's performances can be seen in the ticket office.

* * *

In the mid-1930s, silent movies gave way to talkies, and movie stars performed on stage. By the 1930s and 1940s, shoot-'em-up films, serials, and old film stock were the mainstay for the KiMo movie shows. In 1934, Universal Pictures purchased the film rights to the popular King Features newspaper comic strip, Flash Gordon. The comic strip was created by Alex Raymond and published in 1934 and was later made into a serial film. Flash Gordon was first shown at the KiMo in 1936 and starred Buster Crabbe and Jean Rogers. Originally released on April 6, 1936, "the first thirteen black-and-white episodes ran approximately twenty minutes in length."

- https://www.cabq.gov/culturalservices/kimo/about-the-theatre/history
- https://en.wikipedia.org/wiki/Flash_Gordon

Glass Cases and Memorabilia

The ticket office lobby houses many interesting and educational New Mexican and KiMo history artifacts, none more important than the glass-enclosed, framed picture that announces: "INDIAN SHOW under the auspices of San Felipe de Neri Church, November 18, 19, 20, 1936. P. Clinton Bortell Presents Chief White Eagle and His Company of Inter Tribal Indian Entertainers in An Indian Ceremonial."

Marquee. *Woman of Experience*. Helen Twelvetress and William Bakewell. Circa 1931. Courtesy: Albuquerque Museum and KiMo Theatre.

Other photographs on the walls and behind glass cases announce dozens of movie premieres including: *Little Rascals, Our Gang*, 1930, Hal Roach Studios; *A Woman of Experience*, 1931, RKO Pathé Pictures; *Slave Ship*, 1937, 20th Century Fox Studios; *They Gave Him a Gun*, 1937, Metro-Goldwyn-Mayer; *The Road Back*, 1937, Universal Pictures; *San Quentin*, 1937, WarnerBrothers; *In Old Chicago*, 1938, Twentieth Century Fox; *The Hardys Ride High*, 1939, Metro- Goldwyn-Mayer Studios.

Title: KiMo Parade Float, circa 1935
Creator: Ciotola, Nicholas P.; Timofeyew, Adelina
Subject: Italian Americans; Albuquerque (N.M.)-History; Business enterprises-New Mexico- Albuquerque; Albuquerque (N.M.) -Theaters; KiMo Theatre (Albuquerque, N.M.)
Description: A float promoting the KiMo Theatre passes in front of the theatre during an Armistice Day parade.
(Photo courtesy of Adelina Timofeyew.)
Collection: Nicholas P. Ciotola Italians in Albuquerque Pictorial Collection Institution: Nicholas P. Ciotola Italians in Albuquerque Collection
https://nmstatehood.unm.edu/search/node/KiMo%20theatre

To see the KiMo Theatre parade float, go to:
http://econtent.unm.edu/cdm/singleitem/collection/Ciotola/id/96/rec/1

Posters of Silent Films

The KiMo was not just a movie theatre but also a road house with a stage for burlesque and vaudeville. The walls of the general manager's office are covered with photographs of the early days of the KiMo. One photo on display at the KiMo announces the October 1951 showing of the Metro-Goldwyn-Mayer film *Across the Wide Missouri* with Clark Gable. There is also a poster of the July 1950 film *Duchess of Idaho*, a Metro-Goldwyn-Mayer musical comedy starring Van Johnson and Esther Williams.

Marquee. *The Duchess of Idaho*. Esther Williams and Van Johnson. Circa 1950. Courtesy: Albuquerque Museum and KiMo Theatre.

The Theatre Lobby

On your self-guided tour, after viewing the memorabilia, posters, and pictures in the ticket office lobby, walk up the stairs to the theatre lobby or ask at the ticket office to be let into the theatre through the main doors under the marquee. The KiMo Theatre interior lobby provides visitors with a gateway to cultural and historical information, one of a kind paintings, vistas of the Pueblo Deco décor, the Art Gallery, two unique staircases that lead to the mezzanine and Carl Von Hassler's murals and the doorways into the theatre auditorium.

Gordon Church Portrait

In the lobby, on your left is an oil painting of Gordon Church (1948 to 2006) painted by Leo Neufeld. Church is locally respected as the founder of Albuquerque's Public Art Program which has funded more than 600 pieces of art showcased throughout the Albuquerque. Church worked for the City of Albuquerque from 1978 to 2004 when he retired. For more information on Gordon Church, please watch Anthony DellaFlora's October 2004 video *Gordon Church-A Life in Art* at https://vimeo.com/58053895

Another video KiMo Theatre and Public Art fans recommend is *Making History: Public Art in Albuquerque* which was premiered at the KiMo Theatre on May 11, 2011. The documentary was produced by former Albuquerque Journal reporter Anthony DellaFlora in cooperation with the City of Albuquerque's GOV-TV and the Public Art Urban Enhancement Program. For more information about DellaFlora, Church, Marge Neset, Jane

Sprague, Alan Reid, Sherri Brueggemann, and the history of Albuquerque's Public Art Program watch *Making History: Public Art in Albuquerque* at https://vimeo.com/57236969

Mary McKinney, Popcorn and World War II

For a City of Albuquerque's Cultural Services Department video in May 2012, Craig Rivera interviewed Mary McKinney who worked at the KiMo Theatre from 1941 to 1944.

According to McKinney, in 1941 the cost of admission to the KiMo during the day was 25 cents and 40 cents at night. Popcorn cost 5 cents. McKinney remembers theatregoers could also attend movies at the Pastime Theatre, which she said "became the Chief Theatre," the Rio Theatre, which played so-called "B" movies, the Mission Theatre, where most movies were in Spanish, and the Sunshine and KiMo theatres, both of which showed first run movies.

McKinney chuckled as she remembered when manager Joe Barnett secured a copy of *Miracle on 34th Street* in July and she and her friends sang Christmas songs all summer. During World War II, she said, the KiMo showed war newsreels. "That's how we got our news of our Albuquerque boys." The KiMo Theatre with its Kiva Lo next door became a kids' hangout. McKinney remembers Wednesday night was date night. Kids would meet up at either the "Hi or the Lo," and then go to see a movie.

Marquee. *A Big Shot.* Humphrey Bogart and Irene Manning. Circa 1942.
Courtesy: Albuquerque Museum and KiMo Theatre.

In McKinney's interview, she fondly remembered theatre managers Joe Barnett, Harry Hitchcock, Irving Foy (one of the Little Foy children from the movie *Seven Little Foys*), and her husband, Bill McKinney. She also confessed to Craig Rivera during the interview that she saw a Sally Rand burlesque show.

To watch the entire amazing, delightful, and educational video, please go to: https://www.youtube.com/watch?v=olnzzRAgR18

Continue through the theatre lobby past the art work, past the winding stairs with their ornate wrought iron railing, and enter the KiMo Theatre Art

Gallery. The gallery was added to the theatre during the 1990s renovations. If you don't immediately see the opening to the gallery, you can follow the scent of popcorn which is sold at the concession stand in the gallery during many performances.

Manager Larry Parker describes the KiMo's concession abilities this way. "We have a small food service area and a concession area where we sell popcorn, snacks, and drinks to our patrons. We do have a sink and a commercial refrigerator available to rental groups but we aren't a full service kitchen. The ballet will bring in their own concessions and sales. A group can apply to the City for a license to set up a bar and sell alcohol. Concert promoters often sets up a bar but it is up tothem to apply for a 'Picnic' license. They do the paperwork, bring in the supplies, and the certified bartenders. It's a night by night thing."

Crossover Aisle Drawings

The KiMo Theatre was constructed in 1927 in less than a year. On the walls of the art gallery in what once was a curio shop, you'll find exhibits by local artists. Besides the art work hanging on the gallery walls, you will find a fascinating set of framed architectural plans. These drawings illustrate the architectural evolution of the KiMo.

At the time of its opening, the theatre contained over 1000 seats. As years passed and renovation were completed, the lobby moved into the theatre or auditorium space and a crossover aisle was added. Seating space diminished, and in 2017, there are just over 650 seats.

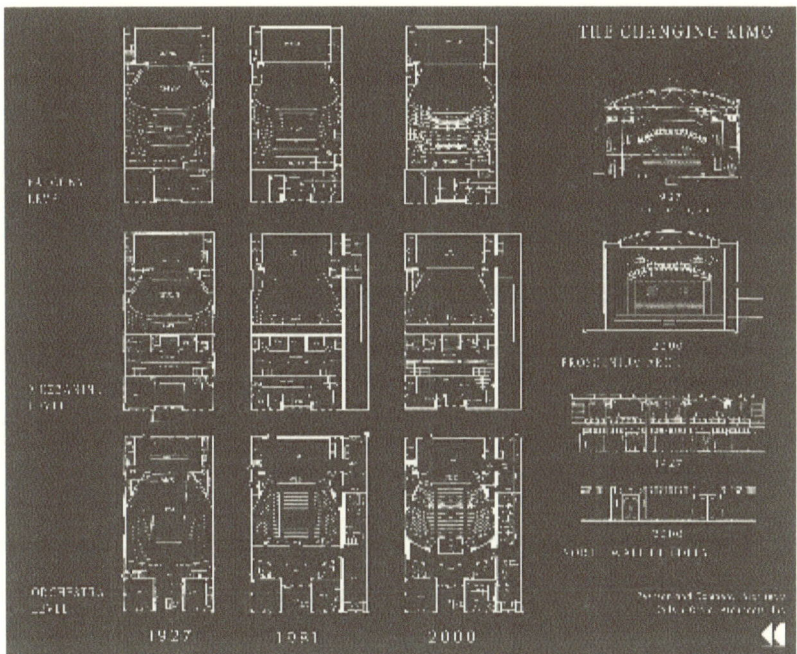

Art Gallery. Architectural plans. "The Changing KiMo 1927 to 2000". Circa 2000. Photo credit: JMLoring.

Painters and Exhibits

Art exhibits are a regular occurrence at the KiMo Theatre. Augustine Romero is the curator of the gallery. Information and guideline criteria for submitting art work for exhibition can be found at

https://www.cabq.gov/culturalservices/kimo/art-gallery-submissions.

Or send proposals to: Augustine Romero, Gallery Curator, 1025 Broadway SE, Albuquerque, NM, 87102. Email: augustineromero@cabq.gov

Sharon Higgins, an Albuquerque painter and muralist, remembers she got a job at the KiMo in 1957 selling popcorn and candy, mostly "So I could see movies."

Fran Krukar, an Albuquerque watercolorist, said about the KiMo's Art Gallery, "My experience with the KiMo is that local art groups have exhibits there in the space off the lobby. I've shown my work. Many times, there was also an artist reception. Well attended. The space also has its own entrance on Central Avenue where a curio shop used to be.

Over the years, I've attended other events. The KiMo holds a classic film fest, I think in the summer, and shows old classics once a week. There have also hosted musical performances that I love. The only story I know about the KiMo ghost is one that I read in the newspaper years ago. The part that sticks out in my mind is the little boy who died there is now a mischievous ghost.

In one instance, all the lights went out during a performance. Someone quickly put a doughnut on the shrine and the lights came on immediately."

Both Higgins and Krukar are members of the Yucca Branch of the National League of American Pen Women. http://www.nlapw.org/

Auditorium. Stage. Circa 1927.
Courtesy: Albuquerque Museum and KiMo Theatre.

The KiMo Theatre Auditorium

Once you have concluded your tour of the Art Gallery, walk back into the theatre lobby, open the doors to the theatre, and enter the auditorium. You may need time to take in the auditorium, carpet, stage, curtain, proscenium arch, Pueblo Deco designs, Native American symbols, Vigas (roof beams) and chandeliers.

If you are visiting the daytime, come back for a performance or movie and see what happens when the lights go out.

The Wurlitzer Pipe Organ

In 1927, the Bachechis spent $150,000 to build the three-story KiMo Theatre building containing a 1000 seat auditorium, and surrounding "profit shops". The KiMo originally hosted movies, vaudeville, and burlesque shows until silent films morphed into talkies and vaudeville and burlesque moved to bars and private clubs.

Rush Dudley said, "In early film history, back when movies began, people thought it was a fad and retained their stages because live performances would come back. That's why old movie theatres had stages as well as screens so they could show movies. Movie theatres were a good place for young people to work as usherettes, ticket takers, and ushers."

In 1927, silent movies required an organ and organist or orchestra to play along with films for atmosphere and affect. Before Warner Brothers. Introduced movies with sound a Wurlitzer pipe organ accompanied films at the KiMo. Occasionally, the organist played a short concert before a film ran. The cost to build the KiMo building was $150,000. Bachechi paid an additional $18,000 to buy the Wurlitzer which was bought and installed during the original 1927 construction.

Auditorium. Wurlitzer organ pipes camouflaged high on the wall to resemble a Navajo rug

Circa 1927.

Courtesy: Albuquerque Museum and KiMo Theatre.

"I have been told that during the 1920s and 1930s, the Wurlitzer was housed on the house right (stage left as actors call it) of the theatre, in front of the first row of seats, before the proscenium arch that separates the stage from the audience. I'm told that it was sold in the 1950s. I may be right or I may be wrong but that's what I've been told," manager Larry Parker said. "In photographs stored at the KiMo, if you look hard, you can see that the Wurlitzer organ's pipes are camouflaged high on the wall to resemble a Navajo rug hung on the east wall by the stage."

According to the text with a photograph archived by the Albuquerque Museum, William Steele Dean was one of the early organists at the KiMo but there is more to his story. The text reads: "William Steele Dean worked at the KiMo Theatre as the organist playing accompaniment for the silent films.

Dean was a silent film fan and would walk the few blocks to the Santa Fe Railway Depot and Alvarado Hotel hoping to take photographs of the famous passengers.

The Santa Fe California Limited spent a little over an hour at the Alvarado Complex, which gave the passengers time to take a break and visit the cafe and Fred Harvey Indian Building. The stop gave Dean time to approach the notable people and with courtesy ask to take their pictures for his scrapbook."

http://www.albuquerquemuseum.org/exhibitions/photo-archives

Wurlitzer pipe organ, pipes, proscenium arch, stage, fire curtain, seats. Circa 1927. Courtesy: Albuquerque Museum and KiMo Theatre

Auditorium. Circa 1990s.
Courtesy: KiMo Theatre. Photo credit: Rush Dudley.

During the 1950s, the original Wurlitzer pipe organ was removed from the KiMo Theatre and began a journey of its own and its story is fascinating. For more information on the manufacture and transportation of the 1927 Wurlitzer organ, who bought the organ from the KiMo, how it ended up in California, and the City of Albuquerque's idea to reinstall the organ to the KiMo, see the link at the end of this section.
https://www.cabq.gov/culturalservices/kimo/about-the-theatre/kimohistory/pipeorgan

Albuquerque Museum Displays KiMo Organ and Ticket Box

From February 25 to August 27, 2017, the Albuquerque Museum showcased an exhibit titled "Hollywood Southwest: New Mexico in Film & Television" which featured dozens of classic movie posters and a photograph of one of the KiMo Theatre's old projectors courtesy of the KiMo Theatre. Other displays at this event included an old, but not the original, KiMo Theatre organ. The plaque with the organ reads: "Organ from the KiMo Theatre, 1940s, Newman Brothers. Courtesy the KiMo Theatre. Gift of the McKinney Family on Behalf of T. Wm. Bill & Mary McKinney."

On display next to the organ was a KiMo Theatre ticket box. The plaque with the box reads: "Ticket box. Wood, brass. From the KiMo Theatre. c. 1927. Gift of Ms. Kathy Schwartzman. PC1979.4.1. Italian immigrant Oreste Bachechi opened the nations only Pueblo Deco Theatre dedicated to Native American culture in 1927."

1940s organ and 1927 ticket box.
Courtesy: Albuquerque Museum and KiMo Theatre.
Photo credit: JMLoring.

Auditorium, proscenium arch, fire curtain.
Circa 1990s. Courtesy: Albuquerque Museum and KiMo Theatre.
Photo credit: Rush Dudley.

The Proscenium Arch

According KiMo manager Larry Parker: "A proscenium is the metaphorical vertical plane of space in a theatre between the actors and the audience. It is surrounded on the top and sides by a proscenium arch that serves as a frame into which the audience views a theatrical performance.

The original KiMo Theatre proscenium arch, including elaborate Pueblo Deco designs, was destroyed in a 1960s fire but was then replicated in the 1970s. Plaster buffalo skulls, turtles, and other Native American symbols were copied from the originals and once again decorate the main proscenium arch. New stage lighting positions were created within other restored areas.

The original grand drape was also replicated and includes medallions and hand-painted details. The entire ceiling in the auditorium was carefully cleaned, repaired, and restored. Conservationists worked for months atop scaffolding far above the auditorium floor to restore the spectacular "environmental" artwork. Vigas (roof beams) decorated with Pueblo Indian motifs seem to open onto a starry night sky. Chandeliers modeled after Native American funerary canoes hang above the audience."

Theatre Fire Curtain

Rush Dudley, remembers, "Since the 1900s, all over the country there were very serious theatre fires where people were killed. All theatres built after that had a fire curtain. When the KiMo had a fire in the mid-1960s, it didn't burn down the theatre because of the fire curtain. And on stages above the actors, there are these special doors or giant vents that open if there is a fire and draw the fire up instead of the fire going out into the theatre.

The fire curtain is between the stage and the audience. The KiMo's curtain was made of thick asbestos that went up and down on counterweights. The curtain covered the whole stage opening. A main curtain is usually decorative, made out of velvet or something. Immediately behind it would be the fire curtain made out of asbestos. That's what the KiMo had and why the whole building didn't burn down in the fire in the 1960s. Fire people showed up, sprayed water, and put out the fire, and demolished the proscenium arch. The Bachechis didn't replace it.

The Bachechi family put up a screen to show movies. That's why in the

1970s all the family did was to show movies. There was very little stage equipment. The fire destroyed the stage proper, but not the walls. After the fire, the family put a new roof on over the stage to keep water out. The organ was long gone when the fire happened. The family sold the organ a few years after the theatre opened."

Continuing Renovations

In the 1930s, when the KiMo showed both silent films and talkies, the Bachechis updated the theatre and wired it for sound. Later, after the 1977 renovations, it became mainly a performance center. In 2018, the KiMo Theatre provides for artistic performances, films, and events the use of state of the art technology.

The $2.5 million renovation completed in 2000 included the installation of new seating and carpet, main stage curtain, new tech both, lighting positions hidden between and behind vigas on the ceiling, and a recreation of the proscenium arch. A new stage ceiling, new rigging hardware, new stage draperies, and new lighting and sound equipment completed the work. Still to be renovated is the stage fly-loft, no longer usable as the result of a 1960's fire, and the older dressing rooms, including backstage plumbing and electrical upgrades.

The KiMo's upstairs business offices were renovated to meet current building and safety codes over the winter of 2000-2001. The third floor office area was renovated in 2002. Work included upgrading plumbing and electrical systems, a new telephone system and new roofing. The auditorium seating capacity was 650 at completion of the restoration in time for 75th anniversary celebration in 2001of Route 66.

KiMo Business office. Circa 2017.
Courtesy: KiMo Theatre.
Photo credit: JMLoring.

Projection Booth, Projector, and Projectionist

In the late 1940s and in the 1950s, the KiMo Theatre was still a movie theatre that showed first-run films and old film-stock footage from a 35-mm projector. One of the two old projectors used at the KiMo is still housed in the projection booth. Another older one was on display on the mezzanine until 2017, when it was lent to the Albuquerque Museum for the exhibit titled. Hollywood Southwest: New Mexico in Film & Television. In 2017, as it did in 1927, the theatre uses the same projection booth housed on the top floor of the building. Projectors have changed from almost room-sized behemoths to a black box the size of a large bread box.

Projector. Circa 1920s to 1950s. Displayed at the Albuquerque Museum on loan from the KiMo Theatre.
Circa 2017. Courtesy: Albuquerque Museum and KiMo Theatre.
Photo credit: JMLoring.

Included among the KiMo memorabilia on display at the 2017 exhibit "Hollywood Southwest: New Mexico in Film & Television" at the Albuquerque Museum was an old projector, a reel canister, and a photograph of the projection equipment and projectionist from the 1940s.

Projection booth. Modern projection system.
Circa 2017. Courtesy: KiMo Theatre.
Photo credit: JMLoring.

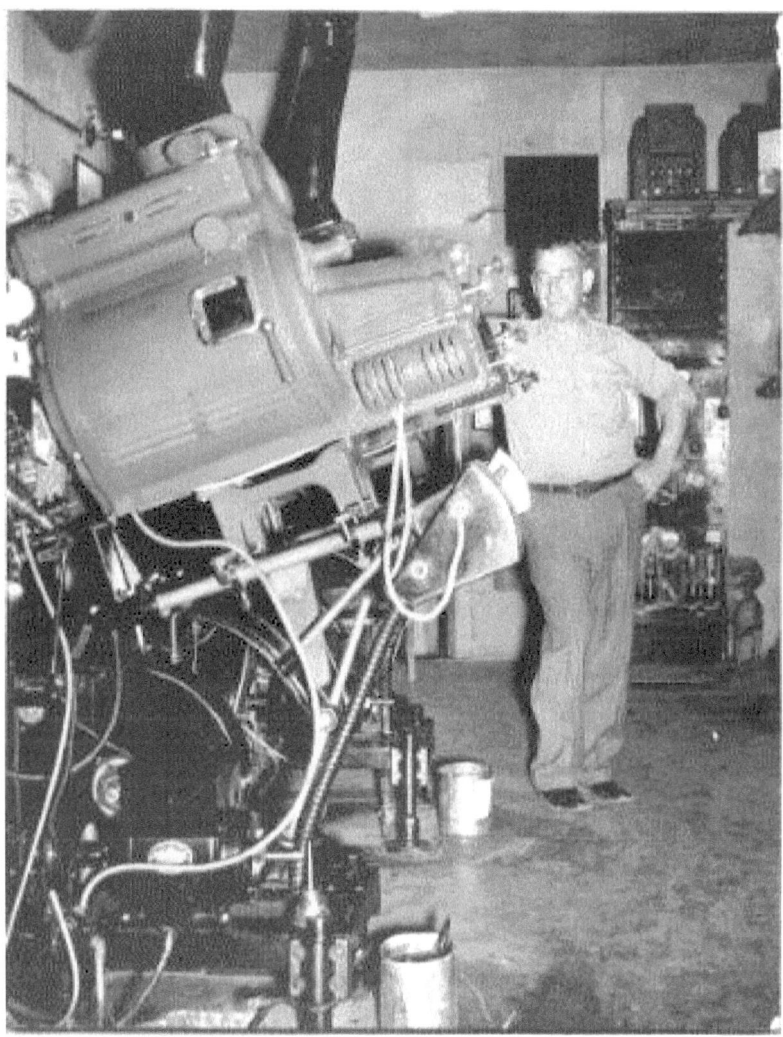

Projection booth, projector and projectionist.
Circa 1940s.
Courtesy: KiMo Theatre

The New Silver Screen

[Editor's note: The following is the text of a press release from the office of former Mayor Richard Berry. Reprinted with permission from Mayor Berry's office.]

Albuquerque, NM, 2012 - Mayor Richard J. Berry today announced the installation of a new "silver screen" at the KiMo Theatre. The screen is one of several additions or changes to the KiMo Theatre during the past several months that have greatly enhanced the experience of attending an event at the KiMo.

The screen was manufactured by Stewart Film screen and does contain real silver particles. The screen, which is about thirty-three feet wide and fourteen feet high, will provide KiMo patrons with a cinema-quality movie experience. With the silver screen, the KiMo will have the ability to showcase 3-D movies as well as archival 35-millimeter films. It also will increase the contrast and brightness of movies.

"When the KiMo opened in 1927, it opened with a 'silver screen,'" said Mayor Berry. "It is great to be able to bring this feature back to this historic theatre, and it is just one of the ways in 2017 that the City is restoring this wonderful building and improving the quality of the experience of coming to the KiMo."

In addition to the screen, the KiMo has received a new coat of exterior paint. The murals in the entryway have been refurbished, and a new HVAC system installed. A new neon sign was installed in front of the theatre this past June [June 3, 2011].
A new sound board and state-of-the art HD projector have also been added.

The first use of the screen will be for a live broadcast of the Academy Award-nominated live and animated short films on Saturday, February 25.
On Sunday, February 26, 2012 the screen will be used to feature the 84th Annual Academy Awards during the Oscar Night America party. The KiMo is one of forty-nine locations in the United States to host an official Oscar Night America celebration. Tickets to this special black-tie event are $25 per person and benefit the KiMo and the Friends for the Public Library.

"Showcasing the Oscars and being the only official location in New Mexico to do so is a KiMo first," said Mayor Berry. "I know it will be exciting and I look forward to seeing many citizens come out to enjoy the Oscar celebration in their Oscar-best. The Red Carpet broadcast begins at 5:30 p.m. Guests will have the

> opportunity to predict the winners of the night's Oscar event in the Nomination Ballot Contest. The person with the most correct predictions will win the grand prize of a tour for two of the set of *Breaking Bad* with City of Albuquerque Film Office director Ann Lerner."

For more information on information in this section, see the following links:

Public art in Albuquerque:
http://www.cabq.gov/culturalservices/public-art

KiMo sign replacement project:
https://www.abqjournal.com/40933/kimo-sign-emphasizes- artistic.html and David Steinberg's article in the *Albuquerque Journal* on July 3, 2011

June 3, 2011, sign dedication gala:
https://www.cabq.gov/culturalservices/public- art/events/dedication-of-the-kimo-theatres-new-neon-sign

Mayor Berry's press release:
http://www.cabq.gov/mayor/news/mayor-berry-reveals-new-2018silver-screen2019-at-kimo-theatre

Theatre Seats - 1971

by Laura Sundt Pierce

Laura Sundt Pierce is the costume designer with the Ballet Repertory Theatre of New Mexico.

Before the City of Albuquerque bought the KiMo and when it had been closed for a while, the homeless had kind of taken over. It was before the cross over aisle was created. I remember The Music Theatre did at least two seasons at the KiMo. I'm pretty sure they did *Man of La Mancha, Oklahoma!,* and *Cabaret.* Those three come to mind immediately. The director was Karl Westerman. There are clippings in my journal.

A friend of mine and I sewed deep covers for the seats. They made a curtain out of strips of fabric. And it didn't look bad, actually. There were dressing rooms stage left where there is empty space now. No dressing rooms underneath the stage. It was quite interesting to take it over, to open up a theatre that hadn't been open for a while. It was community theatre with local performers. There was a live orchestra, I'm guessing between a dozen to sixteen instruments. One of everything you need with a couple of extra violins. Not a gigantic orchestra but enough to fill up the pit. Live music!

The 1971-1972 season of The Music Theatre at the KiMo under the direction of Karl Westerman included *Man of La Mancha*, *Fiddler on the Roof*, and *A Funny Thing Happened on the Way to the Forum*. The 1972-1973 season featured *Oklahoma!* and *Can-Can*. There was a full-page article in the Journal on 9-19-71 about The Music Theatre opening up the KiMo again for *La Mancha*.

Opera Southwest at the KiMo Theatre

According to their web page, Opera Southwest (OSW) produces "world-class opera" and is a "professional regional company producing two to three major operas per year selected from the best of the standard repertoire. To date OSW has produced over 120 major operas for hundreds of thousands of patrons, and are especially proud to have mounted twenty-three world premieres by local composers, including original operas created especially for Albuquerque's children. These smaller operas stress community and educational themes, and have delighted more than 180,000 youngsters with dazzling, exciting, live theatre."

In 1982, Opera Southwest became the KiMo Theatre's premier tenant. Justine "Sally" Tate-Opel (aka Sally Opel) was Opera Southwest's general director. By training, Sally Opel is a stage manager, but for all her years with Opera Southwest at the KiMo, Opel was general director, production manager, and, some folks say, "fully in charge". In 2017, Opel is a board member emeritus along with W. Georg Schreiber.

Accommodating the Opera

By Sally Opel and Stewart Dawson

Sally Opel stated, "Opera Southwest is forty-four years old. I've been with the company for all that time. In the 1970s and 1980s, in the beginning, I wore twelve hats.

Dave Rusk was mayor of Albuquerque back in the late 1970s. [Editor's note: Dave Rusk was mayor of Albuquerque from 1977 to 1981.] He got a grant to build a downtown performance center at the KiMo. In those early days, we were called the Albuquerque Opera Theatre. We changed to Opera Southwest for the 1985-1986 season.

We moved from Popejoy Hall to the KiMo Theatre for our 1982-1983 season. At that time, Dave got the grant to renovate the KiMo. It was an old, semi-dilapidated but gorgeously appointed theatre that was opened as a movie theatre and a roadhouse that was meant for burlesque.

Dave was in charge of the backstage and lobby renovations. He was also the vice president of Opera Southwest's board of directors. So, he knew what was needed to put on an opera. At one time back in the eighties, David got federal money twice to build a downtown performance center. But it was voted down by a poorly worded referendum. And no agreement where to place it. So confusing. They had over $20 million that had to be returned.

One of the things Dave was able to complete while he was mayor was to create the alley way behind the KiMo, the loading doors. Even though it wasn't the space to be used as an active theatre with opera with four sets that needed to be stored somewhere."

Stewart Dawson, lighting, set, and properties designer for Opera Southwest, remembers: "The KiMo wasn't originally set up for grand opera. The ceiling is twenty-five feet high. You could still see where the 1960s fire burned the flyover system. We had to do opera scenes with single sets. Most of the vaudeville shows at the KiMo traveled there by rail spur. Theatres were designed back in the 1920s and 1930s with loading doors that were the same size as a box car, so stuff could be transported. So, you could get scenery in and out the door of a theatre. They built scenery as big as they could fit in the train. Flats were seven-foot-eight-inches in dimension to fit into a box car. They used railroad box cars to bring sets and costumes into Albuquerque. That's why sets were built the size they were. Then the city brought the train in on wheels for the singers' dressing rooms and for them to put on their makeup. They needed to fit everything into the box cars. We stored sets in the KiMo alley and on stage.

In 1985, I think it was, a $100,000 *Faust* production set came off a train," Opel continues, "and it was built for a large company. They didn't want it and they were giving it away. We ended up with a *Faust* production worth over $100,000.

In the 1990s, the public school teachers had something called Character Counts, virtues, cooperation, pride, respect, ways you deal with your life. We wrote operas for children that matched those principles. We often gave special performances of major operas cut down to fit into the hour between school buses dropping the kids off and picking them up at the KiMo. We couldn't put on these productions without Jeff Benham's tech people or the creative talent of Mimi Peavy, our production manager."

"I remember coming into the KiMo after one renovation," Dawson said, "and the orchestra wouldn't fit into the pit. I remember trying to stuff a thirty-five person orchestra into that small space. We had to install a television set so the timpani could see the conductor. The opera made a deal to have the newly installed elevator removed so we could have the space for the orchestra. We had to build a platform over the base because it was up off the floor. The arrangement was that if and when it was a necessity to get to the downstairs dressing rooms the Opera would pay to have the elevator put back in. That was several renovations ago."

Tosca playbill. Albuquerque Opera Theatre (Opera Southwest). 1982-1983 season. Courtesy: Opera Southwest. Photo credit: JMLoring.

The Albuquerque Opera Theatre's 1982-1983 Season

The Albuquerque Opera Theatre in 1982-1983 featured *Tosca* by Puccini, *The Merry Wives of Windsor* by Nicolai, and *Carmen* by Bizet. For the 1985-1986 season, they changed their name to Opera Southwest. The playbill for *Tosca* announced the move to the KiMo Theatre.

With its move to the KiMo Theatre, the Albuquerque Opera Theatre enters its second decade. As the growing regional company, AOT has found its new home in the heart of downtown Albuquerque and expects to play a major role in the continued growth and success of the community's cultural life.

The playbill continues*: We have a more exciting and expanded season for 1982-1983. Our move to the beautiful 'new' KiMo Theatre enables us to offer more and better performances. We hope you enjoy the comfortable seating and better acoustics. I salute the many workers and talented performers for their efforts in bringing quality opera to Albuquerque. Justine (Sally) Opel and James Bratcher, our artistic and musical staff, have contributed greatly to AOT's growth and excellence.* —Jean Smith, President, Board of Directors.

Opel added, "For that 1982-1983 season, we did *Hansel and Gretel* [an opera by nineteenth-century composer Engelbert Humperdinck] and the lights turned off. At that point, no one knew how to run the newly renovated theatre."

Opel said she wrote a grant to the New Mexico Arts Division to hire some people to train to work back stage. Once the KiMo was renovated, it needed a crew of people who knew their craft. "We hired about six people," Opel said. "We had classes for the technical people. We had a technical director on that job and I taught the kids how to run the shows. Glen Kilgore was one of the directors.

We ran our operas and we also produced programs for other people and other arts groups. Stewart Dawson was part of the crew. They have pictures at the Southwest Collection's office and at the University of New Mexico of some of those early productions."

[Editor's note: The collection mentioned above is part of the Southwest Photography Collection, University of New Mexico.]

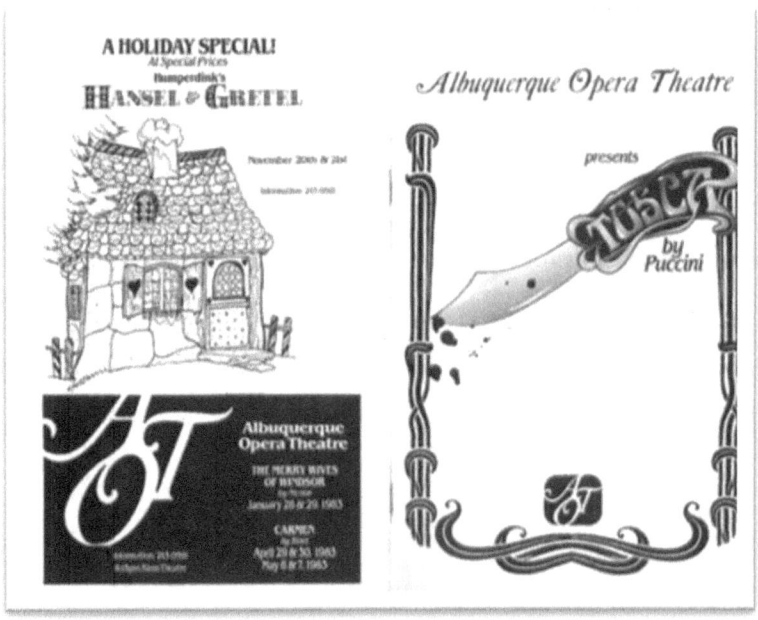

Hansel & Gretel playbill. Albuquerque Opera Theatre (Opera Southwest).
Circa 1983. Courtesy: Opera Southwest.
Photo credit: JMLoring.

AirDance Stage Modifications

by Debra Landau

Debra Landau is the Artistic Director of AirDance New Mexico. She formed AirDance New Mexico in 1995 and produced performances at the KiMo Theatre from 1995 to 1998. According to their web page, "AirDance New Mexico is a collaborative performance company which presents innovative theatrical shows with a special emphasis on the aerial arts."

AirDance was formed as a project under a tax-exempt umbrella in 1995 and we self-produced six shows (four aerial) at the KiMo 1995-1998, inclusive. Our old web page* has a photo of me on an apparatus I made of heavy-duty surgical tubing and latex strips. The picture was shot by Jeff Benham and is from the 1998 show, *Storydancing*.

In 2001, I returned to the KiMo for a show titled, *Vertical Hold*. That production featured a free- standing climbing wall, which is now housed at the AirDance ArtSpace in the South Valley. Audiences are seated with their backs to the climbing wall for recent shows.

The current company, AirDance New Mexico, Inc., was incorporated in 2011 and is its own tax exempt organization.

I loved the KiMo Theatre from the moment I stepped into it as an audience member, a full ten years before I brought my first version of my aerial dance company, AirDance New Mexico, into the historic building to mount a production of my own. I had performed at the KiMo in the interim as a dancer with other companies.

We held five aerial shows at the KiMo, 1995-2001, and the unique and historic nature of the place and the professionalism and cooperation of the staff made each show feel special. Tony Marsh, a certified rigger, was the Technical Director at the KiMo for my first couple/three shows and we worked well together in rigging my trapezes and invented apparatus and trip lines. This was in the early days of both the aerial dance/circus arts boom and the internet, so I made my own equipment and we figured everything out for ourselves.

Yes, there was quite a bit of math involved! In 1997, for a show titled, *By the Twos: Dance and Theatre for the Next Millennium*, we were joined by guest artists Charlene Curtiss and Joanne Petroff. Charlene is a wheelchair dancer and special arrangements had to be made, as she could not access dressing rooms upstairs or down. Charlene is an advocate for the disabled and we like to think her input made it in to the designs for the ensuing renovations that updated the facilities for the disabled.

One downside of the renovation of the KiMo was for AirDance New Mexico's 2001 production, *Vertical Hold*, we had only one obvious beam from which to rig apparatus, cutting through the middle of the stage, upstage to downstage, a problem for multi apparatus dances. Thankfully, with the help of Dennis Potter and more math, we were able to work it out. No matter what I threw at them, as long as I talked it through in advance, the KiMo staff accommodated me, including actual tubs of fire and ice (fire extinguishers at the ready!), a 16' x 12' free-standing climbing wall (not including the front and back braces), and a solo apparatus made of surgical tubing, which we joked was the ingenious equipment by which one could draw and quarter oneself."

www.airdance.org
* http://www.aquilaarts.com/airdancepast.html

Auditorium. Balcony, ceiling, seating. Before proscenium arch renovations. Circa late 1990s. Courtesy: KiMo Theatre.

Auditorium. Stage looking out to seating and balcony.
Circa 1990's. Courtesy: KiMo Theatre.

Stage. KiMo Theatre and Vortex Theatre production of *MacBeth*.
Carpet and seating. Circa 2013.
Photo credit: Rudy Miera

The KiMo Theatre Stairway, Handrail, Balcony, and Mezzanine

by Jacqueline Murray Loring

The KiMo Theatre was built in 1927 and bought by the City of Albuquerque in 1977. That year the theatre was added to the National Register of Historic Places.

From 1977 to 2002, renovations to the KiMo were completed in several phases. The 2002 renovations included replacing flooring and seating, restoring the original Carl Von Hassler murals, modernizing electrical and plumbing, as well as bringing all aspects of the theatre up to building and safety codes and compliance with the Americans with Disabilities Act. The auditorium remained open during most of the renovation time.

Auditorium. 2017 renovation. Seats stacked on stage.
Photo credit: Karen Cunningham.

The 2017 KiMo Theatre renovations included uninstalling, cleaning, and restoring the auditorium seats. The chairs were stacked on the stage and in the art gallery in order to remove the theatre carpet and install new carpet whose print is similar to the design of what removed. The auditorium was reopened for the summer of 2017 for events and programs.

Auditorium. 2017 renovations. Carpet removed. Seats stacked on stage. Photo credit: Karen Cunningham

Auditorium. 2017 renovations.
Above: From stage looking toward production booth and balcony.
Below: Looking west. 2017 renovations. Carpet and seating removed.
Photo credit: Karen Cunningham.

1927 seating and wall artwork.
Courtesy: Albuquerque Museum.

Back in the Theatre Lobby

Dominating the KiMo Theatre lobby are two stairways that lead up to the mezzanine where you will find paintings, posters, and murals that continue to document and enrich the history of the KiMo, Albuquerque, and New Mexico.

Mezzanine. Stairs to balcony.

Circa 1927.

Courtesy: Albuquerque Museum and KiMo Theatre

Above: Mezzanine. Circa 1927.
Below: Mezzanine. Railing. Carl Von Hassler murals. Circa 1999
Courtesy: Albuquerque Museum and KiMo Theatre.

City of Albuquerque Saves the KiMo Theatre

In 1977, Albuquerque voters approved a $324,000 bond to purchase the KiMo Theatre, listed on the National Register of Historic Places. After voters rejected a second bond to provide matching funds to a federal grant for the complete renovation of the theatre, the City of Albuquerque provided $1.1 million for a partial renovation.

Architect Harvey Hoshour and his partner, Dan Pearson, led the first phase of the KiMo's renovation. The KiMo's trademark buffalo skulls were restored to their original colors. Mission light fixtures on the façade were replicated from old photographs. Door handles modeled after Kachinas were duplicated from the one remaining handle.

The balcony railing in the lobby, composed of wrought iron bird figures, was eleven inches too short to meet modern safety codes. Harvey Hoshour devised a novel solution to retain the railings' original look. Additional metal was inserted in the birds' necks and legs to make the railing taller. The talented craftsman who performed the work was none other than the grandson of the man who created the original railing. Another phase of restoration, at a cost of $35,000, focused on the Carl Von Hassler murals.

Friends of the KiMo raised about $10,000, with additional funding contributed by the Urban Enhancement Trust Fund and the Albuquerque Community Foundation. Anne Rosenthal, an art preservationist from the San Francisco Bay area, led the team who worked on the murals. Accompanying her was her husband, Michael Wolfe, and Greg Thomas and Michael Dunn."

— Edited by John Arnold, New Mexico Museum of Natural History,
　　　　　with information provided by the KiMo Theatre.

Text used with permission from:
https://www.cabq.gov/culturalservices/kimo/about-the- theatre/restoration

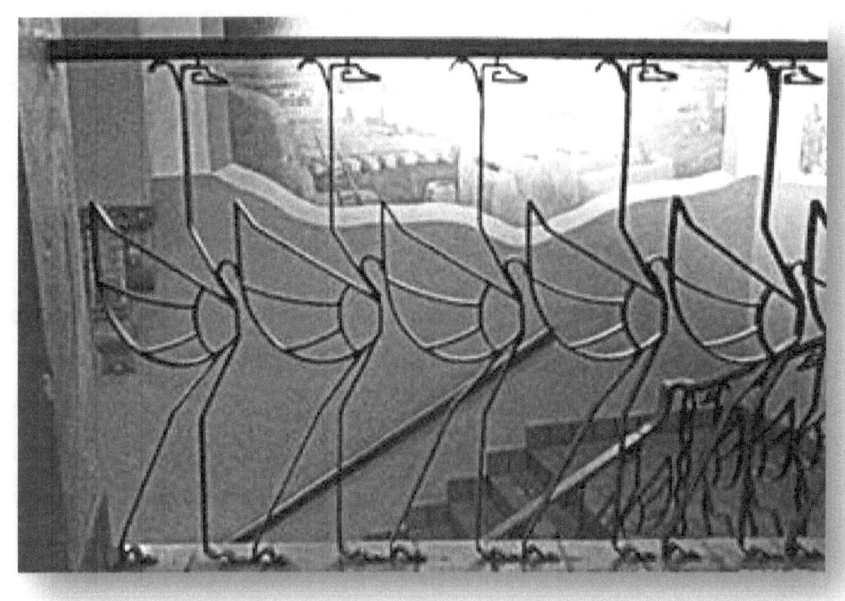

Mezzaninne. Railing.   Renovated birds.   Circa 1999.
Courtesy: KiMo Theatre. Photo credit: Rush Dudley

Carl Von Hassler's Murals on the Mezzanine

In 1927, during the KiMo's construction phase, Oreste Bachechi commissioned painter Carl Von Hassler (1887-1996) to paint nine large murals and two smaller ones depicting the mythical Seven Cities of Cibola using scenic or cultural places of interest in New Mexico. At the top of the stairs on the mezzanine as your eyes adjust to the dimness you will the Carl Von Hassler's murals will reveal themselves behind you.

Von Hassler, known for his landscapes and murals, was provided with a studio on an upper floor of the theatre that was surrounded with windows. Von Hassler and his students built scaffolding on which to stand while they painted the murals in oil directly on the stucco walls. The restored murals are still vibrant. If you are fortunate enough to have your tour guided by Larry Parker, you may have the opportunity to visit Von Hassler's studio. Parker is a valuable resource for KiMo Theatre history and folklore.

Mezzanine. Buffalo heads. Carl Von Hassler's murals.
Circa 1999. Courtesy: KiMo Theatre.

The Missing Carl Von Hassler Paintings

by Jeff Benham

As you walk along the mezzanine past the alcove of posters, you will find a plaque commemorating the lost Carl Von Hassler paintings. The plaque tells the story of what happened to these precious murals. Next to the plaque are Jeff Benham's 1996 renderings of the lost Seven Cities of Cibola paintings. Benham, who worked at the KiMo as a painter, carpenter, and lighting designer tells fascinating tales about the KiMo's "Peacock Room", the year there were two Miss New Mexico's, and the play director who insisted upon using 500 pounds of rice to celebrate a wedding scene. Most "friends of the KiMo" have never heard the actual facts about Benham's renderings of the missing Von Hassler paintings. Benham's secret is an important contribution to the history of the KiMo Theatre. – JMLoring

I worked at the KiMo Theatre from the mid-1980s to 2011, and later for Opera Southwest and the Ballet Repertory Theatre. There were touring groups like Philip Glass and a juggler who juggled twenty balls at one time with his feet.

In the 1980s I worked with folks like Tony Marsh who was the technical director in charge of backstage and Dennis Potter who was technical manager and the assistant to Tony. I think they came on when the city first reopened it, or very soon after.

> 1996 Artist's rendering of missing Von Hassler mural by Jeff Benham
>
> A section of the "Seven Cities of Cibola" murals was destroyed in the late 1930's to create an upstairs window booth for KGGM radio. There are only two partial photographs known of the original mural. Local artist Jeff Benham has created two renderings of the missing mural.

Plaque. Explanation of Jeff Benham's 1996 renderings of Carl Von Hassler's "Seven Cities of Cibola" paintings. Circa 2017.
Courtesy: KiMo Theatre. Photo credit: JMLoring

I remember Debra Landau and her AirDance New Mexico troupe of death-defying performers. The first full AirDance show at the KiMo was probably 1989, maybe a little earlier. We did shows there pretty regularly, once or twice a year, through about 2003 when they got their space going in the south valley.

When I worked at the KiMo, I knew one of Carl Von Hassler's murals in the lobby was destroyed early on. This was done to put a window in the wall where the mural had been. The first radio station in New Mexico broadcast from the KiMo in the room behind where the mural had been. Patrons could watch the live radio hosts while they were in the lobby.

Jeff Benham's rendering of Carl Von Hassler's lost mural. Circa 2017.
Courtesy: KiMo Theatre.
Photo credit: JMLoring.

I was researching the Von Hassler murals when I read an interview that the window was put in when the station began. That didn't seem to match up with anything I found in old newspapers, etc. I just looked it up, and found this link: http://www.oldradio.com/archives/stations/ccs/kob.htm.

The complicated, historical, and legal but educational link, says the station, KGGM, began in 1922 and broadcast from the KiMo in 1941 to coincide with a powerful new transmitter. It wasn't information that was out there when I was researching. I was asked to research the missing mural and create a color rendering of what it looked like. The hope was that at some point this might be recreated on the KiMo wall. When I began, we had two black and white photos of the missing mural. The first showed only the first third of the mural. The second showed the same third plus the middle third, but on such an extreme angle that it was impossible to make out anything more than a few rough grey shapes. When I finished researching several months later, I still had only the same two photos. However, I'd learned a lot about Von Hassler, his style, and the way he worked.

The most recognizable aspect of his work came from his unique pigments, ground from local materials, most notably his blues. I was able to make an educated guess as to what he might have done, and created two versions of what it may have been, believing one was more likely to be in the right realm. This version translated the main grey shape that was extrapolated from the second photo as a figure, and expanded from that assumption.

About a year after I completed the project, on a day that I wasn't at the KiMo, someone in his nineties came by to see the old KiMo while his wife was getting her hair done nearby. He had been one of Von Hassler's assistants on the murals. The staff showed him my two versions and he said he didn't remember it exactly, but that the one that I preferred looked likely to be pretty close to what he remembered.

First Run Movie Posters

by Jacqueline Murray Loring

On the mezzanine there are three recessed walls that display framed posters well worth reading. The posters celebrate the opening of the KiMo Theatre and showcase first-run movie posters. The alcove's posters give valuable insights into the KiMo's first 100 years and reveal a wealth of historical KiMo and Albuquerque history.

Billed in 1927 as the country's most famous "Indian Theatre," the KiMo opened with theatre and street celebrations and the premiere of the silent film *Painting the Town*, with background music provided by the KiMo's newly purchased Wurlitzer pipe organ. *Painting the Town* was a one- hour, black-and-white silent comedy-romance starring Patsy Ruth Miller and Charles K. Gerrard. It was produced by Universal Pictures Corporation. The survival status of *Painting the Town* is listed as unknown.

Parker said, "When Warner Brothers introduced films with sound, it changed everything. The Bachechis found a way to convert the KiMo to sound, so that by the 1930s the theatre showed more sound films than it did silent. By the mid 1930s, it was almost exclusively talkies."

More posters in the mezzanine alcove showcase additional movies including *The Broadway Melody of 1929* which was the first musical released by Metro-Goldwyn-Mayer and the first all-talking musical, but it was also issued as a silent film for theatres without the capability to show talkies. It starred Bessie Love, Anita Page, and Charles King. It was the first sound film to win an Academy Award for best film. It was also nominated for best direction (Harry Beaumont) and best lead actress (Bessie Love). It is best known for featuring two songs, "The Broadway Melody" and "You Were Meant for Me."

On October 6, 1927, Warner Brothers. released its first film with sound. *The Jazz* Singer ran eighty-eight minutes. It opened at the KiMo shortly after its release. The film stared Al Jolson and Mary McAvoy. Jolson sang six songs. *The Jazz Singer* was directed by Alan Crosland, produced by Darryl F. Zanuck, and based on the play of the same title by Samson Raphaelson.

In the early years, the KiMo showed first run movies and showcased many famous entertainers including Tom Mix, star of Western movies, Gloria Swanson, Sally Rand, Ginger Rogers, and Mickey Rooney. Stars like Judy Garland would appear on stage and introduce their movies. In the 1930s, it was also the first home of the Albuquerque Little Theatre, which staged performances there for its first six years. According to Albuquerque Little Theatre's website, actor Vivian Vance, "one of America's most beloved TV personalities," got her start at their first show in 1930.

https://albuquerquelittletheatre.org/about-us/history/

Mezzanine. Poster. Artist A. J. Holder airbrushes Mickey Rooney's face. Circa 1939. Courtesy: Albuquerque Museum and KiMo Theatre.

Mickey Rooney

The KiMo Theatre archive has photos of the opening of *A Midsummer Night's Dream*, where hundreds of people lined up to see this award-winning film. One photograph in the KiMo Theatre's collection shows bicycles piled up along the sidewalk and curb while people waited in line. *A Midsummer Night's Dream* was released by Warner Brothers. in 1935 in black and white and ran 133 minutes. The romantic fantasy that starred James Cagney, Mickey

Rooney, and Olivia de Havilland was nominated in 1936 for four Academy Awards including Best Picture and Best Assistant Director. It also won for Best Cinematography and Best Film Editing.

According to Parker, "Mickey Rooney wasn't on hand for the opening but in later years did make the trip to the KiMo stage." A poster in the mezzanine alcove features a photo of artist A. J. Holder airbrushing the smiling face of a young Mickey Rooney.

Posters and the History of the KiMo
Supporters of the KiMo

Mezzanine. Alcove wall lined with 2002 educational and historical posters. Photo credit: Karen Cunningham.

The mezzanine alcove's posters hold a wealth of historical information, much of it told from personal remembrance and documented research. The alcove's educational posters were created in 2002 by the KiMo Theatre and the Albuquerque Museum of Art and History [Albuquerque Museum]. Research and photos on display at the KiMo were compiled by Sarita Streng.

Text of Educational Posters

The KiMo Theatre opened as a Pueblo Deco picture palace on September 19, 1927, when Art Deco and picture palaces were all the rage. Pueblo Deco was a flamboyant architectural style that fused the spirit of Southwestern Indian cultures with the exuberance of America during the Roaring Twenties.

The KiMo remains the only theatre conceived in honor of the native people of New Mexico. The theatre was the brainchild of Oreste and Maria Bachechi, who immigrated to New Mexico from Italy in 1885. Bachechi chose Carl Boller of Boller Brothers for the design. His friend Pablo Abeita, former governor of Isleta Pueblo, won the award for submitting the KiMo's beautiful name that in the Tiwa language means 'mountain lion' or 'king of its kind: that which cannot be perfected.'

In recognition of the KiMo's architectural and cultural significance, the City of Albuquerque purchased the aging movie palace in 1977, and has since spent over $2 million toward its renovation. With this exhibit, we celebrate over 75 years of joy that the KiMo Theatre—king of its kind—has brought to our lives.

This first poster is highlighted by a photograph of the KiMo Theatre, circa 1927, and the city block where it resided. It offers valuable insight about the KiMo and is grounded and identified with this line of text: "Bachechi Theatre. Albuquerque, NM. Boller Brothers. Architects. Los Angeles, California & Kansas City, Missouri."

The poster is correct for its day, but does not reflect the total amount of money spent on renovations for the KiMo Theatre between 1977 and the 90th anniversary in 2017. According to Dana Feldman, 2017 Albuquerque Cultural Services Director, "The City has spent more than two million since 1977 and easily 2.5 million in 1999 alone. Another one million dollars was spent from 2009- 2017."

Below the picture of the KiMo building is an inserted box that includes a copy of the portraits of Mr. and Mrs. Bachechi found in the ticket office lobby. With the portraits a caption that tells that the photo was taken in "early 1900" and was replicated by the "Courtesy of the Bachechi family."

As you read the remaining posters, historical facts are revealed. You will learn how New Mexico's population grew in the 1920s due to tubercular patients traveling here to convalesce, how in the 1930s movie directors move their cast and crews to New Mexico to make films. There is detailed information about how and why architect Carl Boller divided the building into separate spaces for "profit centers," [Editor's note: professional office space], and a radio station. Read further and discover that during the 1988 renovation the Kronkright Center for Cultural Materials was hired to restore the "original sparkle" to the interior of the building. Keep reading till you find fun facts about the Smoking Room and the Cry Room and how usherettes, ushers, and ticket sellers were required to dress, and the little known but complicated drama of the daily operations of the theatre when it showed silent and early talkie movies.

Albuquerque Museum and the KiMo

At the bottom of one of the 2002 posters, a caption reads: "Organized by the Albuquerque Museum and The KiMo Theatre." On the acknowledgement poster, there is an impressive list of the 2002 KiMo supporters who created the display. You will see the names of Albuquerque people, businesses, government officials, and organizations who believed in the KiMo's past and who contributed to its future.

The End of the Tour

As you end your tour of the iconic, historical KiMo Theatre or head into watch a movie or a performance, take another look at the first poster in the series. Below the 1927 picture of the KiMo Theatre in the inserted box with the portraits of Mr. and Mrs. Bachechi is text that reveals the dream of the Bachechis:

> "...The Bachechis proposed to give the people of Albuquerque a playhouse that should not only combine capacity and comfort but should house the most modern and theatrical facility in a setting of antiquity, one in harmony with the spirit of the Southwest and of Albuquerque. The KiMo is the result."

For over ninety years, the citizens of Albuquerque and New Mexico and tourists from around the country and the world have visited the KiMo Theatre and celebrate it as a performing arts center, a movie palace, and a place for friends to meet and enjoy a multitude of art forms. It is also the symbol of the endurance of the Bachechis dream.

KiMo Theatre. Night performance.
Circa 2017. Photo credit: Brad Stoddard

Acknowledgments

One person does not write a book as important as this one. It was published with the support of dozens of fans of the KiMo. Thank you to all who helped bring *KiMo Theatre: Fact and Folklore* to the hands of readers.

Thank you to the SouthWest Writers 2017 Board of Directors for their faith and support: President: Sarah Baker, Vice President: Rob Spiegel, Secretary: Jim Tritten, Treasurer: Kent Langsteiner. At Large Board Members: Bobbi Adams, Don DeNoon, Dennis Kastendiek, Sam Moorman, Joanne Bodin, Robert Staub, Zachry Wheeler. Class/Workshop/Speaker Coordinator: Rob Spiegel. Social Media and E-lerts: Kim Mitchell. Office Manager: Larry Greenly. A giant round of applause to Webmaster, Sage Editor and 2019 president Rose Marie Kern for her editing and publication support.

Thank you to Peggy Herrington for the foresight to conceptualize the importance of this book and to SouthWest Writers members Brenda Cole and Kathy Wagoner for support in writing the grant. The credit for the richness of the stories included in this book belongs to those who contributed to it. Thank you specifically to SouthWest Writer members: Brenda Cole, Mary Beth Dorsey, Dianne R. Layden, Don McIver, Rudy J. Miera, Sam Moorman, and Kathy Wagoner, Pamela Yenser, Gayle Lauradunn, and Kathy Louise

Schuit for their help. A huge thank you to Linda Jaramillo for her indexing skill and support.

Thank you to photographers, museums, and libraries for allowing their photographs to be included. I want to acknowledge the support of 2018 KiMo manager, Larry Parker. Without his whole- hearted cooperation, his sense of humor, his memory of KiMo Theatre history, and his willingness to share those gems with me this book could not have been written.

Thank you to Mayor Richard J. Berry and the 2017 elected and appointed members of the government of the City of Albuquerque including the 90th Anniversary Planning Committee. Most are detailed in the Planning Committee section of this book.

Thank you to Matthew Carter, Project Coordinator, and the eleven member citizens' committee of Albuquerque's Urban Enhancement Trust Fund, (UETF) (a public endowment created by the Albuquerque City Council in 1983) for their support of the KiMo Theatre. Thank you to Albuquerque City Attorney Eric Locher.

Thank you to author and historian Rudy Miera and his treasure chest of flyers, booklets, brochures, playbills specifically from La Compañia de Teatro de Alburquerque productions and for his generosity to share KiMo and New Mexico history.

I am indebted to Rick Nickerson and Paul Bower of New Mexico Young Actors; Opera Southwest's Sally Opel, Stewart Dawson, Tony Zancanella, and Denise Wernly; and Katherine Guise of Ballet Repertory Theatre New Mexico for sharing their passion for their art and for allowing me to use their photographs.

Thank you to Rush Dudley for sharing his photos, his knowledge of the

KiMo's history, and for helping with my quest to discover the real identities of the folks in the photo I call, "man standing on car." Thank you to Jeff Benham who spent hours with me explaining KiMo Theatre history, introducing me to the long list of KiMo performers, and for sharing the facts behind the lost Von Hassler murals.

Thank you for your support to everyone at University of New Mexico's Special Collections/Center for Southwest Research's Photographic Collections at the Zimmerman Library, specifically: Richard Clement, Dean: College of University Libraries, Tomas Jaehn, Director, Special Collections/CSWR, University Libraries, Amy E. Winter, MPA, Program Specialist, Digital Initiatives and Scholarly Communication, University Libraries and Learning Sciences, University of New Mexico, and the Nicholas P. Ciotola Italians in Albuquerque Pictorial Collection.

https://nmstatehood.unm.edu/

Thank you to the Albuquerque Museum Photo Archives for the use of historic photographs. Thank you to Glenn Fye, Photo Archivist, for his hours of research time. Thank you to Denise Cruse, Communications Manager for her considerations.

http://www.albuquerquemuseum.org/exhibitions/photo-archives

Thank you to: Christina Meisner, Ransom Center Research Associate, Harry Ransom Center, The University of Texas at Austin and Erica Weingartner, librarian, Albuquerque Journal.

My personal and professional thank you to Ramona Galt who read about the KiMo book project in the SouthWest Writers online newsletter "SouthWest Sage" for her editorial expertise.

https://creativemornings.com/people/springbok

The incredible and unique cover art is the work of graphic designer, Michelle Fairbanks, "Fresh Design" https://mfairbanks.carbonmade.com/. Thank you.

The technical and time consuming work of managing the several hundred photographs was done by Terry Hicks. Her patience and willingness to educate me while she worked was greatly appreciated.

Thank you to Anne Sterling for her list of people I "must speak to" and Karen Cunningham for encouraging me to take a new path to find Bachechi heirs.

This book is not written by a member of the Bachechi family. I am indebted to Ekaterina Puccini Timofeyew, daughter of Adelina Puccini, granddaughter of Iole Bachechi and great granddaughter of Oreste and Maria Bachechi for her grace, understanding, good humor, and willingness to speak with me and for sharing her family's stories. I am most grateful to Mrs. Adelina Timofeyew for looking at photographs in an attempt to clear up published "facts" like the one about the pole sitter and Mr. Bachechi.

My deepest apologies to everyone I left out of this book. This project began as a blank canvas.

Everyday a name, face, event, or a date presented itself and set me off on a research quest. At publication, there remains on my desk, a long list of people I did not talk to. Important people who directly or indirectly affected the history of the KiMo Theatre. Forgive me for leaving you out of this manuscript. Please write your stories down. I'm sure there will be another book to celebrate the KiMo's 100th anniversary. Your part in the KiMo story needs to be documented and your impact accounted for.

I can't forget to thank my Cape Cod and Albuquerque cheering sections:

Suzi Reid, Jo-Ann Silvia, Paula Nelson, Anya Achtenberg, and Paul Beck. Thank you to Dr. Daniel W. Junick. And thank you to author Christie Lowrance for reminding me to breathe. A personal thank you to Gary, Lisa, Kendra, Carla, Michael, Robert, Vanessa, ReVaH, Reuben and my sister Norma for allowing me the time and space to write this book. It was an unexpected but worthwhile journey.

-Jacqueline Murray Loring

SOUTHWEST WRITERS

SouthWest Writers (SWW) is a nonprofit 501(c)(3) organization devoted to helping both published and unpublished writers improve their craft and further their careers. Located in Albuquerque, New Mexico, SWW serves writers of all skill levels in every fiction and nonfiction genre. It is 95% supported by membership dues and the fees charged for events. Donations are welcome!

Take a few minutes to browse our website and learn about our anthologies, our classes, workshops, conferences, newsletter and the benefits of membership. Feel free to visit one of our free, twice-monthly meetings.

SouthWest Writers:

- Where you'll hear positive stories about the world of writing.
- You'll be encouraged by your peers.
- Network with a variety of publishing professionals and best-selling authors
- You'll find helpful people in a crowd of friends—and be inspired.

We hope to see you soon!

Other Books by SouthWest Writers

The Storyteller Anthology
The Sage Anthology

www.southwestwriters.com   505-830-6034

Photo by Rose Marie Kern

Author Biography

Jacqueline Murray Loring is a writer, award winning poet, a produced playwright, film maker, and screenwriter. In 2012, she won the Doire Press Irish International Poetry Prize for her collection *The History of Bearing Children*, published in Galway. It won second place in the 2012 New Mexico Press Women award for creative verse. Loring works as a book editor, and book and script consultant.

Vietnam Veterans Unbroken: Conversations on Trauma and Resiliency by Jacqueline Murray Loring was published in 2019 by McFarland & Company Publishers, Inc.   https://mcfarlandbooks.com

Since her move from Cape Cod, Massachusetts in 2012 to Albuquerque, New Mexico she has written/co-written almost a dozen filmed short scripts. Besides writing scripts for produced movies, she has worked as a producer, script consultant and directed one film. Several of her short films have been accepted into film festivals including *Trains, Tracks & Aliens* and *The House on Normal Street* produced by Antonio Weiss. In 2018, she was a finalist in the New Mexico Film Foundation's "Let's Make a Western" contest.

Loring was the executive director of the Cape Cod Writers Center, coordinator of the Eventide Arts Playwriting Competition, and facilitator of the Cape Cod Screenwriters Group. She is the 2018/2019 president of the Yucca Branch of the National League of American Pen Women, and a member of the Arts Foundation of Cape Cod, New Mexico Women in Film and Video, Military Writers Society of America, and SouthWest Writers.

Index

1

1000 Airplanes on the Roof, 68

4

48 Hour Film Project, 15, 94, 163, 164, 173

5

50 to 1, 170

A

A Celebration of Unity, 12, 134, 135, 136, 139
A Funny Thing Happened on the Way to the Forum, 238
A Life in Architecture Annual Lecture Series, 97
A Life in Parts., 168
A Midsummer Night's Dream, 267
A Tribute to Boris Karloff, 179
A Victorian Christmas, 124
A Way Home, 158
A Woman of Experience, 211
A Word with Writers, 5
Abeita, Pablo, 16, 25, 26, 27, 28
Academy Award, 235, 266
Acoma, 22, 191
Aladdin, 120
Albuquerque Arts Board, 205
Albuquerque City Council, 205, 276
Albuquerque Community Foundation., 257
Albuquerque Convention Center, 73
Albuquerque Deco and Pueblo, 171
Albuquerque Film and Music Event, 163
Albuquerque Film and Music Experience, 15, 165, 173
Albuquerque Film Office, 162, 166, 173, 236
Albuquerque Historic Landmark, 204
Albuquerque Journal, 39, 44, 45, 46, 47, 172, 173, 206, 213, 236, 238, 277
Albuquerque Little Theatre, 60, 266
Albuquerque Museum, 25, 31, 32, 35, 41, 42, 43, 47, 48, 49, 52, 58, 62, 70, 99, 105, 175, 191, 195, 203, 206, 208, 210, 212, 215, 220, 222, 223, 225, 226, 227, 231, 232, 254, 256, 267, 269, 272, 277
Albuquerque Museum, 206, 222
Albuquerque Opera Theatre, 77, 240, 243, 244, 246
Albuquerque Peace and Justice Center, 106
Albuquerque Poetry Party, 179
Albuquerque Public Library Foundation, 5
Albuquerque Studios Film & Technology Academy, 96
Albuquerque Then and Now, 171
Albuquerque, City of, 4, 9, 11, 13, 17, 20, 29, 60, 71, 87, 95, 97, 103, 132, 162, 173, 175, 176, 177, 179, 189, 203, 205, 213, 214, 224, 236, 237, 251, 257, 271, 276
Alice in Wonderland, 122, 126
All the King's Men, 179
All-American Parade, 30
Allen, Bukka, 149
Allen, Terry, 149, 150, 152
Allen, Tim, 169
Alloy Orchestra, 173, 176, 179, 206
Alvarado Complex, 223
Alvarado Elementary School, 155
Alvarado Follies, 12, 155
Alvarado Hotel, 63, 64, 223
America's Foremost Indian Theatre, 52, 55, 75, 208
American Institute of Architects, 97, 173
Americans with Disabilities Act, 205, 251
AMP Concerts, 95
Amy Biehl High School, 123
An Evening for Vietnam, 149
Anaya, Rudolfo, 143
Anderson, Joe, 95

Anderson, Laurie, 94
Anderson, Steve, 164
Animal Humane, New Mexico, 166
Annual Feline Film Festival, 166, 173
Anthony DellaFlora, 163, 164, 174
Army of the West, 88
Arnold, John, 190, 257
Arts Board, 205
Asian American Association of New Mexico, 97
Atrisco Heritage Academy High School, 96
Atrisco Land Grant, 27, 135
Atrisco Land Rights Council, 137, 143
Atrisco Pueblo, 134, 137, 138
Ávila, Elena, 143, 144, 145
Ayocuan., 85

B

Baca, Jim, 4, 20, 163
Baca, Jimmy Santiago, 138
Bachech, Oreste, 9, 38
Bachechi, 9, 11, 16, 26, 30, 33, 34, 35, 36, 39, 44, 63, 67, 69, 190, 207, 208, 221, 225, 228, 271, 273, 278
Bachechi Dry Goods, 33
Bachechi, 39, 40
Bachechi, Arthur, 33, 36
Bachechi, Iole, 39, 40, 47, 278
Bachechi, Lawrence, 33, 36
Bachechi, Maria (Mary) Franceschi, 33
Bachechi, Maria Franceschi, 9, 11, 19, 30, 36, 39, 40, 63, 278
Bachechi, Mario, 36, 144
Bachechi, Mary Franceschi, 19, 36
Bachechi, Oreste, 8, 16, 27, 30, 33, 36, 38, 41, 44, 47, 189, 190, 208, 259, 271, 278
Bachechi, Victor, 33, 36, 49
Baez, Joan, 94
Baile folklorico, 68, 87, 123
Ballet Repertory Theatre of New Mexico, 20, 124, 125, 126, 127, 128, 129, 130, 173, 237, 261, 276
Barelas, 87
Barelas Community Center, 87
Barnett, Joe, 33, 214, 215

Bartholomew, David, 158
Batalla, Perla, 68
Bayou Seco, 143
Beaumont, Harry, 266
Beck, Emms, 51
Bellamy, Hakim, 97, 148
Benham, Jeff, 13, 242, 247, 261, 262, 263, 277
Ben-Hur, 179
Benjamin, Rebecca, 81
Bernalillo County, 169
Berry, Richard J., 4, 20, 177, 234, 235, 276
Better Call Saul, 168, 169
Bird, Jenny, 147
Black Culture Night, 73
Black History Month, 178
Blind Boys of Alabama, 69
Bobby, 86, 107, 109, 112
Bodas de Sangre, 82, 88
Boles, Ed, 205
Boller, Carl, 34, 190, 271
Bookworks, 5, 153, 178
Bortell, P. Clinton, 210
Bower, Paul, 12, 20, 117, 276
Breaking Bad, 4, 5, 168, 169, 236
Brown, Greg, 94
Bryan, Pat, 64
Burlesque, 36, 51, 61, 96, 98, 148, 208, 209, 212, 215, 221, 240
Bussey, Rochelle, 161

C

C. J. Box, C. J., 178
Cabaret, 237
Cagney, James, 50, 267
Can-Can, 238
Cannes Film Festival, 165
Carmen, 78, 172, 244
Carter, Jimmy, 76
Carter, Matthew, 205, 276
Central Avenue, 15, 30, 39, 41, 52, 54, 55, 56, 58, 59, 61, 62, 63, 66, 69, 71, 73, 74, 79, 84, 87, 168, 176, 187, 201, 206, 207, 218
Central New Mexico Community College, 106
Chandler Six, 44, 45

Chaney, Lon, 95
Character Counts, 241
Chase, Chevy, 82
Chatter, 97
Chautauqua, 178
Chavez, Denise, 85
Chávez, Jaime, 134, 143, 144, 145
Chavez, Jesús, 86
Chavez, Martin, 133
Chávez, Steve, 143, 144
Chavez-Charles, Margo, 85
Chief White Eagle, 210
Church, Gordon, 213
Cinderella's Glass Slipper, 120
Ciotola, Nicholas P., 47, 197, 198, 277
City of Albuquerque, 4, 9, 17, 20
Civic Plaza, 73
Clarke, Alan, 20, 67, 68, 71, 73, 77
Classical 95.5 KHFM, 96
Cline, Patsy, 62
Cole, Brenda, 3, 11, 33, 51, 275
College of St. Joseph, 81
Columbia Pictures, 207
Consulate of Mexico, 98
Coppelia, 130
Copperman, Neal, 95
Cormier, Dr. Steve, 178
Coronado Center, 63
Country Dreaming, 115
Crabbe, Buster, 209
Cranston, Bryan, 167, 168, 178
Crowell, Rodney, 94
Cruse, Denise, 277
Cultural Services Department, 97, 203, 205
Cunningham, Karen, 252, 269, 278

D

Darnall, Bobby, 12, 86, 107, 108, 109, 110, 111, 112, 114, 119, 127, 158
DATA Charter High School, 97
Davidson, Jolianna, 121
Davis, Daniel, 97
Dawson, Stewart, 13, 108, 240, 241, 245, 276
Day of the Dead, 90, 140, 141, 144, 145
DeGrassi, Alex, 68

de Haviland, Olivia, 50
de Oñate, Don Juan, 87
Dean, William Steele, 222
DellaFlora, Anthony, 12, 95, 163, 164, 174, 213
Dell'Amore, Alexandra, 21, 186, 187, 199, 200, 202
Department of Cultural Affairs, 121, 178, 205
Dia De Los Muertos, 141, 143, 142
Die Fledermaus, 78
Disney Channel, 169
Dobrusky, David, 115, 120
Don Quixote, 86
Doña Tules, 86
Dorsey, Mary E., 12, 155
Dorsey, Tommy, 62
Douglas, Stafford, 120
Downtown Albuquerque, 9, 29, 63, 72, 73, 74, 77, 79, 82, 84, 92, 177, 181
Downtown Saturday Night, 73, 74
Doyle, Virginia, 39, 47
Doyle, Virginia Puccini, 40
Duchess of Idaho, 212
Dudley, Rush, 5, 11, 12, 20, 29, 43, 44, 62, 67, 85, 108, 127, 131, 192, 221, 224, 227, 228, 258, 276
Duke City, 45, 88
Duke City Shootout, 12, 15, 163
Dunn, Michael, 257
Duranes, 84

E

Ehecatl Aztec Dancers, 11, 90, 91, 123, 145
Ehecatl, 144
El Rey Theatre, 39, 40, 59
El Sueño de Navidad del Santero, 146
El Sueño del Santero, 84
Encinias, Dr. Miguel, 88
Eubanks, Kevin, 167
Events Planning Division, 177

F

Fairbanks, Michelle, 2, 278
Fat Sam's Grand Slam, 115

Faust, 78, 241
Feldman, Dana, 104, 176, 177, 203, 271
Feline Film Festival, 166
Ferris, Mark, 176
Fiddler on the Roof, 238
Fields, Doris, 143
film projector, 104, 206, 231, 232, 235
First National Bank, 29
Flejtuchovich, Harlughe E., 85
Flicks on 66, 163
Fox, Benny, 44, 45, 46
Foy, Irving, 215
Fractal Foundation, 97, 173
Franciscan Hotel, 63
Frank, 170
Frankenstein, 94
Freed, Max, 76
Fresh Design Books, 2
Friends of the Public Library, 153
Fright Night, 95
Frontier Restaurant, 69
Fye, Glenn, 41, 277

G

Gabaldon, Diana, 5
Galloway, James, 158
Garcia, Rodrigo, 5
Garcia-Camarillo, Cecilio, 143, 144
Ghost, 86, 107, 108, 109, 110, 112, 172, 218 ,107
Giese, Katherine, 12, 20, 124, 125, 126, 129
Gilbert and Sullivan, 3
Glass, Philip, 68, 261
Gold, 170
Golden West Saloon, 39
Gonzales, Manuel, 147
Gordon, Flash, 209
Gordon, Roxy, 149
Gorman, R.C., 87, 91
Graebner, Jim, 164
Greene, Ethan, 158
Greyhound Soul, 149
Griego, Lauren, 68
Gromelski, Dennis, 164
Gunn, Sue Ann, 158

Guthrie, Arlo, 94
Gutierrez-Hubbell, 27

H

Hagerman, Jim, 149
Haimovitz, Matt, 40
Hal Roach Studios, 211
Hammond, Kaylee, 118
Hansel and Gretel, 244
Harry Ransom Center, 277
Harvey, Fred, 64, 223
Hassler, Carl Von, 13, 99, 204, 213, 259, 260, 262, 263
Haydar, Mona, 5
Herrington, Peggy, 275
Higgins, Gareth, 5
Hillerman, Anne, 4, 5, 12, 153, 178
Hispanic Cultural Center, 158
Hispanic Heritage Night, 73
Hitchcock, Alfred, 53
Hocus Pocus Magic Show, 98
Holder, A. J., 267, 268
Holiday, Billy, 178
Hollingsworth-Marley, Brenda, 178
Honk, Jr., 120
Horn, Paul, 68
Hoshour, Harvey, 75, 77, 257
Hot Heels, 47
Howard E. Roosa Papers, 59
Hughes, Kahlila, 97

I

In Old Chicago, 211
In Plain Sight, 169
INDIAN SHOW, 210
Indie Q, 15, 163
Inskeep, Cheryl, 130
Integrated Control Systems, 96
Irizarry, Harry, 97
Isleta Pueblo, 20, 25, 26, 27, 35, 63, 134, 135, 137, 138
Isleta Pueblo, 26, 27, 134
Italians in Albuquerque Pictorial Collection, 47, 197, 198, 277

J

JAWERKS, 95
Jimmy Awards, 121
Johnson, Janae, 148
Jojola, Lloyd, 39
Jolly, Jeff, 96
Jolson, Al, 266
Jones, Buck, 207
Jordan, Tracy, 3

K

Keaton, Buster, 176, 179
Kern, Rose Marie, 2, 275
Keshet Dance Company, 94
KGGM, 53, 58, 263
Khalife, Marcel, 94
KHFM, 96
Kilburn, Mark, 85
Kilgore, Glen, 245
King, Charles, 51, 266
King, Michelle, 176
Kinney, Harry, 66, 68, 79
Kirtland Air Force Base, 61
Kiva Hi, 50
Kiva Lo, 214
Kronkright Center for Cultural Materials, 271

L

La Bohème, 78
La Compañía de Teatro de Alburquerque, 11, 81, 82, 83, 84, 85, 87, 88, 91, 132
La Mancha, 237, 238
La traviata, 158, 159
La Zarzuela de Albuquerque, 68
Langner, Barbara (Babs), 172
Langston, Liz, 164
Las Posadas, 85
Launch Pad, 95
Lawrence, Martin, 169
Layden, Dianne R., 12, 17, 103, 275
Legendary Locals of Albuquerque, 66, 172
Lemonade Mouth, 169
Leno, Jay, 167
Lerner, Ann, 162, 164, 177, 236

Lew Wallace Elementary School, 130
Lewis, Irene Olever, 83
Library, 25, 35, 277
Little Rascals, Our Gang, 211
Looking In, 96
Lopez, Jessica Helen, 148, 179
Lorca, Federico García, 82, 88
Loring, Jacqueline Murray, 1, 2, 11, 14, 15, 19, 38, 59, 61, 134, 161, 251, 265, 279, 280, 281
Los Griegos, 84
Lost Tribes Productions, 138
Love, Bessie, 51, 266
Lugosi, Bela, 95
Luna, Nita, 143
Lúnasa, 94
Luz, Consuelo, 179
Lyons, Stewart, 168

M

Macbeth, 86, 188
Macy, William H., 169
Madame Butterfly, 78
Man of La Mancha, 237, 238
Manx, Harry, 149
Marge Neset, 68, 73
Marigold Festival Parade, 141
Marsh, Tony, 68, 248, 261
Martin Short, Martin, 82
Martin, George RR, 5
Martin, Steve, 82
Martinex, Padre José, 86
Martinez, Demetria, 147
Martinez, Jesús "Chuy", 144, 147
Martinez, Margarita, 82, 85, 87
Martinez, Patrice, 82
Mathews, Dave, 176
Mayor Berry, 95, 173, 206, 234, 236
McClellan's Five & Dime, 72
McIver, Don, 12, 147, 275
McKean, Michael, 168
McKinney, Bill, 215
McKinney, Mary, 60, 214, 215, 225
McLean, Don, 68
McNally, Shannon, 94

Megill, Joshua, 118
Megill, Lee, 118
Meier, Johnnie, 205
Meisner, Christina, 277
Meloy, Chris, 176
Melzer, Richard, 66, 172
Metro-Goldwyn-Mayer, 211, 212, 266
Metropolis, 206
Miera, Rudy, 64, 80, 81, 83, 90, 91, 134, 135, 136, 138, 139, 140, 141, 142, 143, 144, 146, 172, 250, 276
Miera, Rudy J., 6, 11, 20, 85, 87, 89
Miller, Trish, 170
Miracle on 34th Street, 214
Moncure, Joseph, 148
Mondragón, Jerry, 143, 144, 145
Mondragon, Lieutenant Governor Roberto, 87
Monroe, Bill, 69
Monroe, Marilyn, 95
Moorman, Sam, 13, 193, 275
Morrelli, Christine, 172
Mountain Bell, 73
Movies & Meaning Festival, 5
Murals, 70, 204, 251, 259

N

Nakai, R. Carlos, 94
Napoleone, Mrs. Armida, 33
National Endowment of the Arts, 121
National Historic Landmarks, 204
National League of American Pen Women, 173, 219, 281
National League of American Pen Women, 281
National Poetry Slam, 147, 148
National Register of Historic Places, 204
Native American Night, 73
Navajo, 94, 104, 190, 191, 197, 222
Navajo Nation, 190
Nazi, 104
Neset, Marge, 68, 73, 213
New Hope Full Gospel Baptist Church, 96
New Indian Theatre, 33
New Mexico Arts Division, 85, 245

New Mexico Dance Company, 109
New Mexico Department of Cultural Affairs, 205
New Mexico Film Foundation, 3, 4, 148, 281
New Mexico Film Office, 94, 161, 173
New Mexico Museum of Natural History, 190, 257
New Mexico Philharmonic, 94
New Mexico Post Alliance, 3, 70, 108, 166, 167
New Mexico Post Alliance, 167
New Mexico School for the Arts, 154
New Mexico State Centennial, 207
New Mexico State Register of Cultural Properties, 205
New Mexico Veteran's Memorial, 175
New Mexico Young Actors, 113, 115, 117, 118, 119, 121, 122
Nickerson, Rick, 12, 20, 113, 114, 115, 120, 121, 132, 276
Nob Hill, 30, 84, 105
Noble Shropshire, 88
Norris, Dirk, 4
Not Fit for Man or Beast, 114
Nuestro Teatro, 84
Nuevo Mexico, Sí!, 81, 82, 86, 87, 88, 91

O

Occupational Safety and Health Administration, 131
O'Connor, Kathryn Kennedy, 60
Odenkirk, Bob, 5, 168
Office of Senior Affairs, 178
Oklahoma!, 237, 238
Old Town, 29, 172, 175
Old Town Albuquerque, 84, 106
Oliver-Lewis, Irene, 85
Oñate's Lament, 88
Opel, Sally, 13, 68, 132, 239, 240, 276
Opera Southwest, 12, 108, 145, 157, 158, 159, 239, 240, 241, 243, 244, 246, 261, 276
Oscar Night, 235
Outpost Performance Space, 97

P

Page One, 153
Page, Anita, 51, 266
Painting the Town, 265
Paintings, 13, 143, 261
Palm de Grease., 163
Palmer, Mo, 171
Parker, Larry, 5, 14, 20, 25, 61, 64, 94, 98, 104, 108, 168, 174, 176, 188, 205, 206, 216, 222, 227, 259, 276
Pass Time Theatre, 57, 214
Past Time Theatre, 33
Pastime, 19, 36, 38, 39, 59, 214
Pastime Theatre, 19, 214
Pat Graney Company, 68
PAZ, 91, 123, 144
Pearson, Dan, 257
Peavy, Mimi, 242
Peone, Nikki, 176, 177
Perryman, 150
Perryman, Deryle, 149, 150
Philharmonic, 94
Philharmonithon, 96
Pieerce, Laura Sundt, 237
Pippi Longstocking, 120, 121
pole sitter, 11, 44, 47, 278
Popejoy Award, 121
Popejoy Hall, 77, 240
Potter, Harry, 94, 179
Presley, Elvis, 62
Preston, Douglas, 178
Prohibition, 56
Projector, 206, 232
Proscenium arch, 93, 220, 222, 223, 227, 228, 229, 249
Public Art Urban Enhancement Division, 205
Puccini, Luigi, 39, 47
Puccini, Oreste, Jr., 40
Puccini's Golden West, 39, 40
Pueblo Deco, 3, 104, 144, 150, 154, 171, 213, 220, 225, 227

Q

Quezada, Steven Michael, 4, 169

R

Rainosek, Larry, 69
Rand, Sally, 54, 207, 208, 209, 215, 266
Reagan, Ronald, 76, 84
Reggio, Godfrey, 5
Reid, Suzi, 279
Rhodes, Rick, 12, 17, 103, 105, 106
Rigoletto, 78
Riker, Bill, 106
Ringling Brothers and Barnum & Bailey Circus., 40
Rio Theatre, 59, 214
Rivera, Betty, 97, 205
Rivera, Craig, 205
Rodriguez, José, 81, 82, 84, 88
Rogers, Ginger, 54, 167, 207, 266
Rollins, Henry, 94
Rooney, Mickey, 3, 54, 87, 266, 267, 268
Roosevelt, Teddy, 27
Rosenthal, Anne, 257
Route 66, 3, 15, 56, 93, 150, 167, 187, 205, 206, 229
Rusk, David, 11, 20, 64, 67, 71, 240

S

Sadaqah, 97
Sainte-Marie, Buffy, 94
Same Same But Different, 149, 150
San Felipe de Neri Church, 210
San José, 84
San Quentin, 211
Sanchez, Archbishop Roberto, 87, 92
Sanchez, Tomas, 170
Sandia Mountain., 62
Sandia Pueblo, 63
Santa Fe California Limited, 223
Santa Fe Opera, 131
Santa Fe Railway Depot, 223
Schreiber, W. Georg, 239
Schueler, Chris, 96
Schwartzman, Kathy, 225
Secord, Paul R., 171
Sephardic Jews, 179
Seven Cities of Cibola, 197, 259, 261, 262

Shakespeare, 3, 196
Shields and Yarnell, 69
Sí, Hay Posada, 83, 84, 85
Silent films, 177
Silver screen, 15, 163, 234
Slave Ship, 211
Smith, Alexander McCall, 5, 178
Smith, Jean, 244
Smith, Patricia, 143, 147
Solis, Danny, 147
Somé, Malidona, 5
South Broadway Cultural Center, 176
Southern Slam Dance Group, 180, 181
Southwest Burlesque, 96
Southwest Research and Special Collections, 197
Southwest Shootout, 147, 148
SouthWest Writers, 2, 15, 17, 18, 33, 93, 149, 172, 174, 193, 275, 277, 281
SouthWest Writers Workshop, 2
SouthWest Writers, 18
Space Between Us, 170
St. Marie, Buffy, 3
Staples, Mavis, 94
State Theatre, 59, 72
Stevens, Brent, 96
Stoddard, Brad, 3, 14, 20, 166, 167, 188, 202, 274
Stover, Police Chief Bob, 75
Streng, Sarita, 269
Stringer, Alan, 158
Sunshine Theatre, 29, 59
Suttle, Clark, 96
Sutton, Amanda, 5
Swan Lake, 125
Swanson, Gloria, 54, 207, 266
SWSO, 148

T

Taj Mahal, 68
Tamarind Institute, 105
Tarde de Oro, 178
Tate, Robert, 115, 120, 158
Teatro Consejo's Pachuco Angels Dance Review, 143

Territorial Fair 1890, 29
The Age of Innocence, 179
The Ballet Repertory Theatre of New Mexico, 124, 126, 130, 237
The Broadway Melody, 266
The Detectives Who Loved Opera, 172
The Fall and Rise of Champagne Sanchez, 6, 172
The General, 176, 179
The Good, the Bad and the Cuddly, 166
The Hardys Ride High, 211
The Hours, 179
The Jazz Singer, 266
The Long March Tour, 94
The Lost Pueblo, 170
The Magic Mrs. Piggle Wiggle, 120
The Magnificent Andersons, 179
The Merry Wives of Windsor, 78, 244
The Music Theatre, 237, 238
The New Mexico Humanities Council, 178
The Old Man and the Sea, 179
the orchester pit, 127, 158, 237, 242
The Road, 179, 211
The Underground Nutcracker, 69
The Waltz of the Governors, 88, 91
They Gave Him a Gun, 211
Thomas, Greg, 257
Thorogood, George, 68
Three Amigos, 82
Ticket office, 56, 187, 189, 207, 209, 210, 213, 271
Timofeyew, Adelina, 11, 38, 39, 43, 44, 278
Timofeyew, Ekaterina Puccini, 39, 40, 43, 278
Tingley Beach, 30
Tiwa, 22, 23, 25, 26, 27
To Kill a Mockingbird, 179
Torrez, Angie, 85
Tosca, 78, 243, 244
Toya, Steven, 180, 181, 182
Travolta, John, 169
Treasure House books, 153
Tricklock Company, 97
Twentieth Century Fox, 211
TwoBricks, 149

U

Underground Nutcracker, 69
Unitarian Universalist Fellowship, 106
Universal Pictures, 209, 211, 265
University of Albuquerque, 81, 84, 88
University of New Mexico Zimmerman Library, 207
University of New Mexico, 277
Urban Enhancement Trust Fund, 203, 276

V

Vance, Vivian, 54, 94, 266
vaudeville, 36, 54, 61, 114, 115, 208, 209, 212, 221, 241
Vega, Suzanne, 94
Vicious Circles, 178
Vietnam veteran, 149, 150
Vigil, Dr. Cipriano, 178
Von Hassler, Carl, 13, 70, 99, 104, 105, 190, 197, 204, 213, 251, 256, 257, 259, 260, 261, 262, 263, 264, 277
Vortex Theatre, 3, 250

W

Wagoner, Kathy, 12, 13, 61, 63, 93, 197, 275
Walker, Alice, 5
Ward-Osborne, Travis, 120
Warner Bros, 221, 265, 266, 267
Watermelon Mountain Jug Band, 20, 65, 66, 88
Watson, Doc, 69
Weingartner, Erica, 277
West, Sarin, 120
Westerman, Karl, 237, 238
White, Walter, 168

Wild Hogs, 169
Williamson-Teller, Verna, 20, 26, 27, 134, 135, 137
Winrock Shopping Center, 63
Wolfe, Michael, 257
Women of the World Poetry Slam, 148
Woodson, Jacqueline, 5
Working Classrooms, 133, 145
World War II, 61, 69, 104, 193, 194, 214
Wurlitzer organ, 13, 34, 70, 221, 222, 223, 224, 265
Wurlitzer pipe organ, 223

X

Xiukwetzpaltzin, Mapitzmitl, 14, 90

Y

Yenser, Kelly, 150, 151
Yenser, Pamela, 12, 149, 150, 275
Yescas, Florencio, 90
You Were Meant for Me, 266
Youth Developmental Incorporated, 133
Youth Diagnostic Center, 88

Z

Zamora Rita, 123
Zamora, David, 12, 123
Zancanella, Tony, 12, 157, 158, 276
Zanuck, Darryl F., 266
Zeon Signs, 205
Zia Pueblo, 181
Zimmerman Library, 203, 277
Zuni language, 22
Zuñi Lullaby, 88

www.ingramcontent.com/pod-product-compliance
Lightning Source LLC
Chambersburg PA
CBHW020417010526
44118CB00010B/299